Margaux

BERNARD GINESTET'S GUIDE
TO THE VINEYARDS OF FRANCE

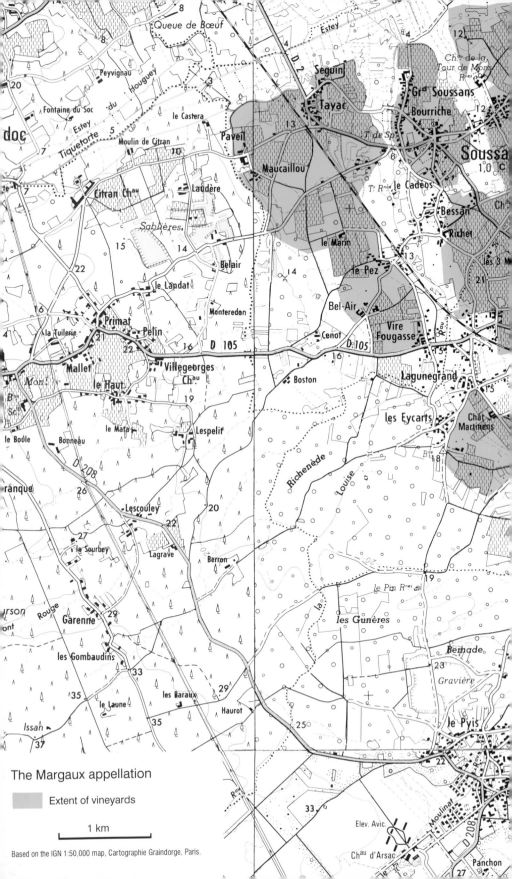

The Margaux appellation

Extent of vineyards

1 km

Based on the IGN 1:50,000 map, Cartographie Graindorge, Paris.

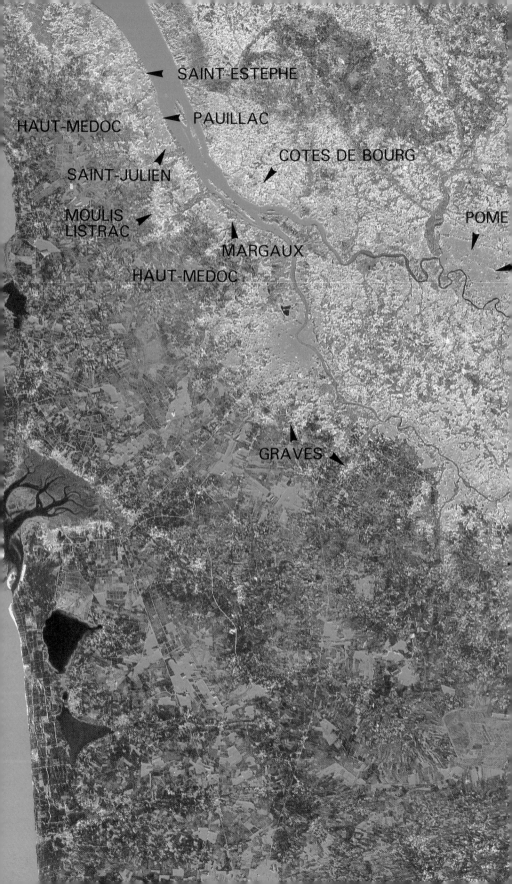

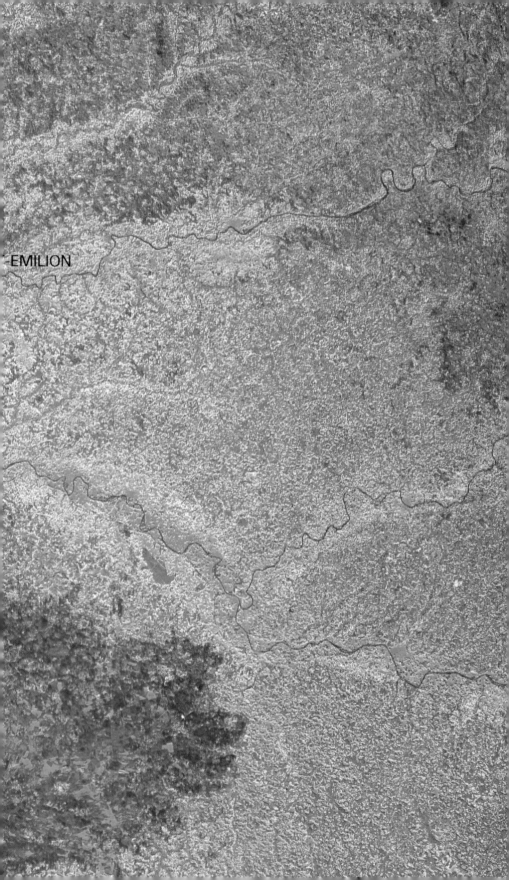
EMILION

Bernard Ginestet

Foreword by Hugh Johnson

Margaux

Translated by John L. Meredith

BERNARD GINESTET'S GUIDE
TO THE VINEYARDS OF FRANCE

Jacques Legrand

Originated and produced by:

Jacques Legrand SA

English version edited by:

Editor:	Nicholas Faith
Assistant editor:	Tamara Thorgevsky
Translator:	John L. Meredith
Copy editor:	James Lawther
Editorial secretary:	Christine Fourton
Art director:	Henri Marganne
Layout:	Claire Forgeot

© 1989 Jacques Legrand SA, Paris
for the French edition
© 1990 Jacques Legrand SA
for the English edition
Distributed in UK by Longman
Distributed in Canada by Raincoast Books

ISBN 0-582-07540-8 for Longman UK distribution
ISBN 2-905969-35-0 for the rest of the world

Printed in Belgium by Brepols, Turnhout

Dear reader...

"We claim to represent a style of living whose values stretch out way beyond our frontiers," declared the President of the Republic, Georges Pompidou, on February 15, 1970, when he was on a visit to Washington. At the time, the aptness of this statement struck me. Applying its sense to one specific field, I have often used it as a sort of slogan for the wines of France. It is undeniable that the French style of living is intimately linked to wine, the supreme expression of all that this style embodies. To try to divorce it from our culture would be unthinkable, and abroad it firmly upholds our image as a civilized nation. This idea should doubtless be extended to take in all the arts of the table, and knowledge of wines should perhaps be included in the science of gastronomy; but the wine-lover's aesthetic feelings are distinguished by their cerebral content. Wine's initial appeal is of course to the senses, but this is rapidly transformed into intellectual delight. Although it is perceived subjectively, it is also a powerful agent for communication, and if only because of this it assumes an important place among the aspirations of our contemporaries.

The true lover of good wine also has a thirst for culture. He seeks to know, the better to love. The book which you have just opened belongs to a collection which sets out to define a new art of wine, or more precisely, a new approach to the understanding of it. It is a worthy undertaking.

Foreword

The range and focus of the discussion of wine over the last ten years or so has been like a zoom lens dissolving a crowd scene to pick on a granule of the big picture. From the days when Lichine's The Wines of France *was considered a pretty specialized book, publishers moved, not at all long ago, to regional volumes on Bordeaux, Burgundy and the other famous vineyards. With this series wine-scholarship takes the logical next step: it focuses on the commune as the unit, at the same time narrowing the focus and allowing us a far greater insight into its components, its methods and motives.*

There is a more microscopic view still: that of the individual property. Premiers crus *and other lordly estates with long histories are suitable subjects for such treatment, but not on the whole the wine-growing property of the middle to upper rank, whose historical peculiarities are less important than their present-day make-up and morale. For them it seems eminently appropriate to take the communal view: close enough to enjoy the detail, but distant enough to make useful comparisons.*

This series differs in another, perhaps even more important way from the great majority of books about wine. Most authors review the subject from the standpoint of a more or less disinterested observer and consumer. This makes them strong on comparison – at any rate superficially – but often weak on insight. Bernard Ginestet is an author who addresses the world from the very heart of his theme. He is a passionately involved insider in Bordeaux, a man who has made a score of vintages, has dealt in the biggest stakes in the business as proprietor of Château Margaux, has participated in the manoeuvres of the market as a négociant. *A man not to be fooled: enthusiastic, yes, but not starry-eyed. Steeped as he is in the region, he cannot hide his feelings for long. Sometimes they are written on the lines, sometimes between them. Always, even behind some seemingly bland report, you feel the beat of the author's pulse.*

Facts and statistics are the bare bones of the books. No detail of encépagement, *of vinification, of production or availability or soil; no label, no telephone number even is omitted. The flesh on these bones is history, anecdote, and above all experience.*

The story starts with the physical and historical groundwork, including new geological maps in fascinating detail. The heart of the introduction is the gastronomic question – what is the identity of this appellation? How do you recognize its wines? How do its citizens view them, use them, and marry them with local ingredients in local dishes?

The repertoire of châteaux follows, leaving nothing out: a piece of research of inestimable value that goes far beyond any other document I know in its scope, even leaving aside the author's deep involvement with his subject. It does not attempt to be particular about wines and vintages. This is not a book of tasting notes – rather the book that enables you to taste with discrimination; to know what it is you are tasting and to draw accurate conclusions. The single consistent conclusion that the author draws is the rapport qualité-prix, *or value-for-money, indicated by a row of glasses. The more full glasses, the higher his rating.*

The photographs, specially commissioned for the series, do not need my encomiums. I need only say that each volume can teach you more about each commune than would a dozen visits without such a guide.

Hugh Johnson

For Vincent, Stéphanie and Mathilde

Contents

The curious and sometimes amusing history of the deservedly famous "Margaux" appellation

If by chance you should wish to taste a good cross-section of Margaux wines without having to pay too much for such a whim, try to strike up a friendship with a fireman from Margaux. By tradition, the annual banquet of Sainte-Barbe (the patron saint of firemen) is held on the first or the second Sunday in December. Three of the twenty-one voluntary firemen are designated as volunteers to look after the wines. After High Mass, the procession makes its way to the War Memorial, where a wreath is laid and the majorettes perform to the rhythmic accompaniment of the brass band called "Prestige Margaux", led by its young director Pascal Nouaux whose mother and father work on the vines at Château Margaux. Then comes the distribution of the certificates and medals, the thanks from the head of the fire brigade and the mayor, the speeches of the Deputy if he is present and the County Councillor who never misses this event. After the aperitif, given in honour of the important personages present, and the ever tricky business of placing the guests at table, the banquet can begin.

Beforehand, during the course of one or two training manoeuvres, the fire-fighters have carried out an inspection visit in the neighbouring cellars. Each proprietor has put by a case of bottles. If only from the wide variety of wines it contains, Margaux fire-station's cellar is one of the best in the commune. The menu is adequate! For example:

Fish soup
Oysters with sausages
Wild boar stew
Guinea fowl flambéed in cognac
Dauphine potatoes
French beans
Green salad
Cheeseboard
Black Forest gâteau

Wines from Margaux

Coffee – Liqueurs   17

The wines will follow one after the other for a good five hours, from one to six o'clock. Their bouquet, colour and taste are considered and discussed. There are different vintages. They are compared. They are evaluated. The diners recall what the weather did during the year in question: "You know, the year there was the fire at old Joseph's place... — It's true, it was cold at the beginning of May in 1974. A fearsome May moon brought on sharp frosts every morning for at least five days — Especially over by Virefougasse — Yes, but Virefougasse doesn't have a Margaux appellation — Are you sure? — Certain — But they make good wine — Yes, but only in the good years — Anyway, it's more in Soussans — That's not Margaux — Here, taste this Marquis de Terme — By comparison with the Lascombes I find it more subtle — That's because it's older — Ageing counts, old boy — I almost prefer the Larruau — That's young Chateau's wine — Bernard Chateau — It's rather comical to be called *Chateau* in Margaux! — Yes, but he makes good wine, all the same — And very good wine, too — Let me have a taste — After, we'll try the Rauzan-Gassies — Hey! Francis!... Pass the Rauzan-Gassies over — At any rate, this year it's been a good harvest — Yes, you're right. It's been good this year, hasn't it Father?"

"The Parish of Margaux lies on a plain on the left bank of the Gironde, from which the church is but five hundred yards away. The terrain of Margaux is composed of very good gravelly soil and accordingly, extremely good wines are made there which are highly appreciated. Those of the Château are so famous that they have been sold for as much as 100 louis per tonneau. The land of this parish which borders the river consists of a large stretch of very beautiful, fine meadowland. The principal produce of Margaux is wine.

"This parish is bordered on the east by the river Gironde, on the west partly by the parish of Soussans and partly by that of Cantenac, on the south side, by this latter and on the north by Soussans. Margaux is twelve miles distant from Bordeaux and approximately five from Castelnau. There is a post office for light mail, which assures a daily distribution of letters except on Sundays. The parish is about five miles in circumference; the village called le Doumench, which is the furthest away from the church, is only a thousand or so yards down the road. The King's highway which leads from Bordeaux to Pauillac and from there into the Lower Médoc crosses this parish from south to north.

"There are two ports in Margaux, one called the King's Port and the other which bears the same name as the parish. This belongs to the Lord of Margaux and is hardly used any more, being badly silted up and it will not be long before the other is put completely out of service
18 *because of sandbanks which have built up in front of it and made*

access very difficult. Before the formation of these sandbanks, the two ports of Margaux were very busy. There was a minimal amount of trade in corn and flour in the parish to supply its own needs and those of the surroundings, but that does not alter the fact that the principal occupation of its inhabitants is vine-growing."

Margaux still has a priest. But since the writer-priest Baurein's *Variétés bordelaises* in 1784, the port of Margaux no longer sees any "trade in corn and flour". But that does not alter the fact that the principal occupation of the inhabitants is still vine-growing and that the fame of its wines is still as renowned as in the eighteenth century.

It was from the years 1720-30 that the vineyards of Margaux established their fame once and for all. Vines had been cultivated there since the early Middle Ages. Yet the idea of *grand cru* was as yet unknown, and trade was not firmly established. It was more or less the same throughout the whole of the Bordeaux region, and certainly in the Médoc where, with one or two rare exceptions, the mushrooming of châteaux started in earnest after the reign of Louis XIV. Formerly, a few lords and rich landowners had the main part of the vine-growing land divided out amongst themselves, the vines nearly always being leased out to peasants.

So, every family of vignerons was allotted the responsibility of a handful of plots of land which local custom measured in "journals", that is the size of vineyard a man could work in one day. Harvesting was then done separately from plot to plot and vinification took place directly in *tonneaux*, each containing approximately 9 hectolitres, which also served for ageing and transporting the wine.* The wines then differed from one grower to another. More often than not, they were identified by the "parish" they came from. So wines from Cantenac were distinguished from those of Margaux. But for each particular area, there was a certain individual flavour which the merchants called "type". In his excellent book *Le Goût du vin*, Professor Emile Peynaud considers that the "type" of the wine is an idea created out of nothing by the wine trade. My modest opinion is rather different. Even if the English word "type" comes near to its explanation, the original meaning of this term in the professional sense of the Bordeaux trade tends to cover all the characteristics describing a wine coming from one given area. I will have occasion to come back to this point later.

---

* *The "tonneau" is a theoretical measure still used in Bordeaux. It is equivalent to four hogsheads of 225 litres each of which gives 300 bottles of 75 centilitres. In fact, losses and wastage reduce the quantity of bottles, called "frontignans", from any one tonneau to 1,152. But more frequently today, the* grands crus *are sold by cases of twelve.*

Etymologically speaking, right up to the end of the seventeenth century, there was a whole host of wines in Margaux (just as in Sauternes, Pomerol, Pommard, Rivesaltes, etc.). In order to choose from this variety, the brokers used to scour the countryside, taking vast numbers of samples which they presented to the fine palates of the great Bordeaux business world. The terms and conditions of each deal, namely each cask, were the subject of a transaction by a method which our contemporary telephones and telexes have consigned to the obscurity of a distant age. Over the centuries, *"cru"* and "type" changed meaning. But it is easy to play with words of this type, each one according to its own *cru*.

The nobility of the *ancien régime* were not wrong. You can say what you like – and say it again: blue blood could appreciate red and white wine. So much so that when certain members of the nobil-

---

▲ *Before entering the village of Margaux from the direction of Bordeaux, you can see the parish church on the right. It was formerly the private chapel of Château La Mothe, the ancient name of Château Margaux. On the left is Château Abel-Laurent which today is one of the estate's out-buildings.*

ity saw the purple-coloured wine which so brilliantly enriched their pourpoints, they gave their name to the produce of their land. So a profusion of casks (labels were printed later) were stamped with the family coat of arms of marquises, counts, viscounts, barons, who walked the corridors of the Louvre or the Parlement de Bordeaux under the concupiscent gaze of future royalist poseurs of the Revolution. So we saw such names appear as "Bel-Air, Marquis d'Aligre", "Marquis de Terme", "Durfort, Comte de Vivens"... followed each century by yet more noble families. In Pauillac there were the Rothschild barons and in Margaux the Count of Saint-Exupéry, the Baron de Brane and the famous banker Pillet-Will who is particularly remembered for being proprietor of Château Margaux and, to honour the second half of the twentieth century, the "High Pontiff" of wine, the late Alexis Lichine, previously converted into the Father Prior of Château Prieuré-Lichine.

Together, the trade and the great families were to develop the idea of *cru* such as exists nowhere else in the world. And here I must stress that this task was achieved by their combined efforts, a fact which has been rather overlooked today. Members of the nobility were not merchants. On the other hand, the nobility served as a blazing pro-   21

motional and public relations' beacon long before *Vogue* magazine came out. It was backed by the Chartrons wine trade, flattered by this economic symbiosis and able to speculate on the competitive upward struggle for prestige in which the lordly suppliers engaged, rather like race-goers betting on thoroughbreds and their jockeys.

It was in this intense atmosphere of friction that another Hundred Years War took place (in round terms, between 1750 and 1850). It could also be called the "War of the Châteaux". For then the producers who put in an appearance on their estates only two or three times a year, mostly at harvest-time, could not forgo an outward display of their wealth... however precarious it may have been. It was a real case of psychosis: château-mania or the "build-on!" syndrome. Some demanded height, this being measured by the number of storeys and keeps, pinnacles, towers and turrets. Others, perhaps with a keener sense of awareness, wanted a succession of halls, suites, and corridors to the innumerable "guest-chambers". Several more privileged – wealthier – ones set about satiating their hunger for façades in three dimensions. The result of all this today is a baroque conglomeration of grandiloquent edifices in which the neo-Gothic and Renaissance architects vie fiercely with one another. But at the same time, the vineyards were being organized, the cellars were being enlarged or reconstructed, the vat-houses were being equipped with presses, crushers and huge fermentation vats. The face of viticultural estates, as we know it today, was taking shape. As regards "ancient" châteaux, that is those predating the seventeenth century, the only one which exists in the Margaux appellation is Château d'Issan, situated in the commune of Cantenac. The actual term "château" to indicate a *cru* is quite recent. At the time of the 1855 classification, only Lafite, Margaux, Latour, Issan and Beychevelle were designated as châteaux. The others simply took the name of the principal locality of the estate, sometimes followed by the name of the proprietor as we have seen further back (it should not be forgotten that labels were very rare, being more often than not printed by the despatching merchants or the consignees).

So it is easy to mock today's use of the Bordeaux term "château" whether in the Médoc, Sauternes, Graves or anywhere else. Some journalists take a delight in doing so and, starting with Mauriac and

◄ *Objects, tools and works of art having a bearing on grapes and wine are highly prized by Médoc châteaux owners. A bacchante on the grounds of Château Lascombes.*

The façade of Château Margaux has served to illustrate practically every work concerning Bordeaux wine since the nineteenth century. This is a little known Italian engraving dating from the Second Empire.   ▶

continuing through to the châteaux, they decry Bordeaux snobbish-ness. Indeed, it is an old and chronic story. "Be a vigneron and get yourself noticed!" wrote the late Pierre-Marie Doutrelant in *Les Bons Vins et les autres*, and he continued: "It means you own a château, towers and gold-rimmed china tableware. It means you put rose bushes at the end of every vine row. It means throwing dinner parties. You hunt and dance, and have thirty *retainers* who by them-selves manage to make the good wine of the year. It means you sell this wine and especially its mystique!" This view of the viticultural world of the Gironde is false. The original meaning of "snobbish-ness" is "lacking in nobility". Pierre-Marie Doutrelant forgot that the true *raison d'être* of the viti-vinicultural nobility is the *vineyard*. The growers and their *retainers* are grafted onto this reality to infuse life into it. They own a château because the château exists. It is often adorned with towers. It is not essentially to get themselves noticed that they repair the roofs. They plant flowering rose-bushes at the end of the rows because it is more attractive when you are strolling round, and the *retainers* prunes and sprays them in the same way and at the same time as the vines. The gold-rimmed china tableware goes well on white tablecloths which do not distort the colour of the wines. It is a family heirloom which has come down from mother's grandfather and it is a nice way of honouring friends who come to dine. And what was the rest?... Are hunting and dancing, when the opportunity presents itself, unseemly pastimes for those who sell good wine and good living? Pierre-Marie Doutrelant reminds me of R.-J. Courtine (La Reynière) going into ecstasies about pickled pork with lentils along with a red Bouzy, and decrying the indecent pre-tension of a great Médoc wine, decanted into a crystal carafe by the sommelier in a famous three-star restaurant. Is he hoping to break into the mystique?... that of the grumblers,* perhaps!

Château Margaux is the centre-stone, or, if you prefer, the liq-uid Regent of this river of *grands crus* which stretches out over the five communes of the Margaux appellation. What is particularly re-markable about it is that it actually bears that name. Sometimes this is a source of confusion on wine lists, yet this same-sounding name brings about other benefits. The world-wide fame of Château Mar-gaux brings a dazzling lustre to the fame of Margaux and through it, to all its *crus*. Conversely, the diffusion of this name on the labels of six dozen properties of the Margaux AOC spreads wide a fame

---

For several years, R.-J. Courtine wrote articles on gastronomy in the magazine Cui-sine et vins de France *under the pen-name of "Convive grincheux" (The Grumbling Guest).*

which reaches consumers of all types. From the north to the south: Soussans, Margaux, Arsac, Cantenac and Labarde form and continue the Margaux appellation. But Margaux is also a postal district (postcode 33460) serving nine communes. Viticulturally speaking, Macau to the east and Arcins, Lamarque and Cussac-Fort-Médoc to the northwest are totally divorced from Margaux as far as the *appellation d'origine contrôlée* is concerned. Whether they are "Bordeaux" or "Bordeaux supérieur" or "Haut-Médoc", the wines produced in these four communes have the name Margaux on the label only for the purpose of their postal address. I admit that it is sometimes difficult for the profane to find their way in this labyrinth of local customs. But to complicate things even further, within the perimeter of the "Margaux AOC" communes, there are fields which do not have the right to the appellation. These are either sandy heaths situated mainly to the south of Arsac and Cantenac, or recent clayey alluvial deposits bordering the river which are known as *palus* (e.g. the Domaine de l'Ile-Margaux is an isolated stretch of silty land by the Garonne, straddling the communes of Cantenac and Margaux, and produces only straightforward but dependable *Bordeaux supérieurs* wines). So then the words:

Margaux
Appellation d'Origine Contrôlée

or else:

Appellation Margaux Contrôlée

(which are exactly the same) have a precise meaning indicating high quality compared to the other hundred-and-one possible uses of the name of Margaux on a label or for publicity, headed note-paper... and invoices from a person despatching the wine, be he producer or merchant.

The Margaux AOC was created by a law dated August 10, 1954. The other great Médoc appellations were already in existence. Last but not least, as we say, Margaux arrived... In point of fact, it was a difficult and painful birth, after a fifty-year pregnancy during which the growers of Margaux and the surrounding areas had waged a fierce battle concerning the different districts.

Even long before this present conflict, the parishes of Margaux and Soussans were at daggers drawn. As early as the fifteenth and sixteenth centuries, each of the priests of Saint-Michel in Margaux

---

Opposite Château Rausan-Ségla is one of the best stretches of this poor gravelly land which is so typical of the Margaux terrain, on which it is practically pointless to use herbicides. ▶

and Saint-Romain in Soussans used to set his respective flocks at loggerheads, sometimes even, for the good of the cause, in league with the sorcerers of the two villages, who at full moon would release black hens onto the neighbouring vineyards in order to wreak the worst possible destruction on the future harvest. At Rogationtide, this holy war sometimes took an ugly turn. The processions, leaving early in the morning, used to go round the countryside, halting at the temporary altars erected in front of the farms and at the foot of the crucifixes which marked the crossroads on the country lanes. On the tables spread with embroidered cloths, a few flowers and pious statues accompanied the offerings of victuals destined for the Good Lord to invoke his clemency on the flocks and harvests. The procession was followed by a cart loaded with this earthly food. What became of it later was not to be asked of the priest. One of these lanes was predestined for trouble for it was the boundary of the two parishes. Several incidents had occurred over the centuries. In 1592, three days before Ascension Day, the two processions from Soussans and Margaux came face to face through an unfortunate conjunction of circumstances, the secret of which was known only to the Devil. There was no question of either one or the other retracing its steps, for the narrowness of the road made it impossible for the two to pass comfortably alongside each other. This was the sign for the start of invective from the cross-bearers and the men carrying the banners, shouted out in colourful local dialect. Then the altar-boys, delighted by this demonstration of local patriotism, began to fight bitterly with their opposite numbers, and the ladies exchanged blows with the help of prayer-books. The sacristans then engaged in a duel with holy-water sprinklers, encouraged by their respective priests who elevated the tone of the dispute with curses in Latin. That evening in Margaux and Soussans, there was many a painful bruise and many bloody trews. And since that time a chronic animosity has entwined relations between the two villages; it still remains deep in everybody's memories of the communes' history.

So from the beginning of this century, there has been a string of lawsuits between the growers of Margaux and those of Soussans, the former wanting to prevent the latter using the name of Margaux to designate their wines. Things became more complicated because several *grands crus classés* in Margaux owned vines in Soussans. How could they prevent the use of an appellation which they themselves

---

Beside the brook called La Louise, in the commune of Soussans, the Tower of Bessan bears witness to the violent history of wars "when the English harvested in Aquitaine"

(as the title of the popular book has it). ▶

were using for similar products? The Association of Margaux Proprietors, founded in 1923, was set up to protect and defend the name of Margaux. After many long wranglings, it succeeded in obtaining a declaration whereby "the wines from the commune of Soussans do not have the right to the Margaux appellation and that this being a final judgement, the matter should never again be called into question, even with the support of new documentary evidence". As for the rest, the conclusions were subtle: "It is an entirely different question to know if the Margaux proprietors who have land outside the commune can have the right to this appellation, or if this appellation can be accorded to the proprietors of neighbouring communes, complete strangers to Margaux." The old widow Domench de Celles sparked things off for at the beginning of the century, she claimed to call her production "Margaux wine", this coming from the estate on the Ile de Fumadelle, situated on the riverine limits of the commune of Soussans. After this, there was a certain Clauzel, a proprietor at Avensan, who was charged with unauthorized use of the name of Margaux. In 1919, a group of communes was already chanting together in unison. Without renouncing their identity, they all wanted to make Margaux wine. There were not only the communes which today have the Margaux AOC but also Arcins, Avensan, Listrac, Moulis and Le Pian. That was flinging the cork a bit far.

For a time, the conflict became as much like that of Clochemerle as that of the war of the processions. All these passions were embodied in the firm of the Braquessac family, who lived in Margaux where they also had their cellars, and who owned "only 3,000 vine plants over an area of 80 ares in the parent commune as against 3 hectares in Soussans, 7 in Cantenac and 30,000 vines including a number of hybrids" (report of the Anti-Fraud Department, November 12, 1936 and memorandum of the court records dated November 4, 1937). In short, they were "proprietors in Margaux" but their authentic "Margaux" wine had the proportions of lark pâté (you take one lark and a horse and you mix them...). Against their will, the Braquessacs became the scapegoats of the most distinguished jurists of Bordeaux. Local politics took a hand and the Margaux town council became a party to the action "to support its official, Monsieur Braquessac, with the reservation that there be no financial charge on the commune of Margaux". This did not prevent their losing the case both at the Court of Appeal and in the High Court.

To cut this long story short, and in spite of the "final judgement", it was the *crus classés* round Margaux which saved the appellation. The layout of their holdings according to the Land Register was complicated: it overlapped the communes of Margaux, Arsac, Cantenac,

Labarde and Soussans. It would serve the interest of none of them to destroy the corpus of the land it owned even if this were represented by a group of different parcels dotted about here and there. Desmirail, Marquis de Terme, Giscours, Cantenac-Brown and a few *crus bourgeois supérieurs* harvest round about Arsac. No *cru classé* has its principal building in Soussans but the majority of the Margaux *crus classés* have land there. Indeed, does not Château Margaux itself have extensive vineyards in Cantenac and Soussans?

Five years before the official classification of 1855, Féret and Son, publishers at 15, Fossés de l'Intendance in Bordeaux, brought out a book by Charles Cocks, A *Foreigner's Guide to Bordeaux, Its Surroundings and Wines, Classed in Order of Merit.* (This book is the forerunner of all the editions of *Bordeaux et ses vins,* which is commonly known as *Le Féret.*) Here are his comments on the five communes in question:

"Arsac: Part of the land, namely the pebbly gravel slopes, produces wines which are full-bodied and firm, with a fine colour and delicate bouquet; they rather resemble those of Cantenac and Margaux, and can be bottled after five years.

"Cantenac: Its soil, white, black and sandy, is a very good gravelly type with a high pebble content. Its wines are sappy and because of their high quality rival those of the best communes of the Médoc, especially by their bouquet and their nutty mellowness which particularly distinguish them; they are also full-bodied and have a fine colour.

"Labarde: This little commune occupies a very picturesque position. Vines are all that is grown there to any extent. Its sandy, gravelly soil produces a better wine than that of Macau. It is remarkable for its charm, colour and bouquet.

"Margaux: ...produces the best rated wines in the department. Once these wines have come to maturity, they are extremely subtle, have a fine colour and a very suave bouquet which fills the mouth; they are generous without being heady, they quicken the stomach yet respect the head, and leave the breath unsullied and the mouth fresh. Their reputation is widespread throughout Europe.

Half-butts, known as "douils", arriving at the vat-house of Angludet. A mobile block and tackle carries them to the crusher-stemmer. Vinification begins. ▶

"Soussans: Although this commune is so close to Margaux, its wine does not enjoy the same fame, despite the fact that the *premiers crus* of the commune of Margaux and in particular Château Margaux itself have huge stretches of vines there. The wines of Soussans are powerful, sappy and have a rich colour. But they are also rather hard, which prevents these qualities from developing before the sixth year of their life."

Cocks's comments, largely inspired moreover by William Franck who published his first *Traité sur les vins du Médoc* in 1824, clearly differentiate the respective qualities of these five denominations... without giving too much offence to anybody. They attempt to define the "types" of each terrain considered as a communal entity. And that is just where the trouble lies. However moral its intentions may have been, the law concerning the appellations of origin followed this route and relied too heavily on the administrative boundaries of the communes, whereas the real idea of origin comes from the geology, climate and the agrology of the area. Of course this origin has to be given a name (Margaux or not Margaux, that is the question). It is certain that all these quibblings had their origin in the outstanding reputation of Château Margaux. So the great appellations of Saint-Julien, Pauillac and Saint-Estèphe, to name but these, were easier to define than Margaux. And if Lafite, Latour and Haut-Brion had been names of parishes, all the local parishioners and those of the surrounding areas would have wanted to claim to take the Sacrament together at the same High Mass. (It should be noted that wherever there is a nondescript locality such as La Fite or La Tour on the Land Register, its owner never fails to mention this on his label and to sell his wine dearer than his neighbour does. As for Mouton-Rothschild, it is disloyal to itself, producing a rival with a test-tube baby called Mouton-Cadet.)

As we have seen, the problem of the postal address is quite distinct from that of the appellation, though inextricably linked to long-established local practices. It arose, in a different but comparable way, at the time of the railway revolution in France and the Médoc. Today, Margaux station is no more than a modest halt on the "Chemins de fer économiques du Médoc", a humble and costly subsidiary of the National Railways on the line from Bordeaux to the Pointe de Grave: the extreme north of the Médoc. But at the time when the steam-horses reigned over communications and commerce, this was not the case. Every Friday evening, wealthy Bordeaux families used to arrive at Margaux station to spend the weekend on their estate. The team of servants would be waiting for them, amid a confusion of shouts, bells, stamping of horses and cracking of whips. The generation which knew the end of the nineteenth century has now died out. As a child, I was lulled to sleep, in the true sense of the term, by these descriptions, always the same, told over and over again. But at the time, casks were also despatched by rail, so supplanting the river barge-traffic, while the ports of Issan, Margaux and Soussans were being left to silt up.

Because the commune of Cantenac did not have the advantage of a station of its own, the railway activity of the two communes was concentrated in Margaux, so much so that the mayor of Cantenac sent a request to the mayor of Margaux, that "Margaux station should bear the name of Margaux-Cantenac". After being put to the vote on August 28, 1892, the mayor of Cantenac's proposition was rejected by nine votes to three. In May 1896 with the municipal elections, there was a change of mayors and town councils. The commune of Cantenac renewed its request. It was "considered". On May 23, 1897, Margaux's municipal council confirmed the preceding ruling, justifying its decision in the following way:

"Seeing that it is not out of simple caprice that the commune of Cantenac wishes to associate its name with that of the commune of Margaux but from the hope of benefiting from this association; that the proof thereof is that this commune formulated the request in August 1892 and that, having duly debated, the town council of Margaux was overwhelmingly against it;

"Seeing that the reason for this request is easy to understand, that although the name of Cantenac is held in esteem in the wine trade, it is in fact Margaux which has pride of place; that it enjoys world fame, that the misappropriation of this name by sellers of mediocre products harvested everywhere, even in California [sic], arises from this fame, highly instrumental as far as wine sales and profits therefrom are concerned; that accordingly it is not surprising that the growers of Cantenac wish to link the names of Margaux and Cantenac as a sort of publicity operation;

"Seeing that, if this link gave rise to an advantage to the growers of Cantenac, it would necessarily be to the disadvantage of Margaux;

"Seeing that, if the commune of Cantenac regrets that its name does not feature in railway guides or on notice-boards and signs on the Médoc line stations, it cannot logically ask that its name be linked to that of the nearest station; for in that case, it is the name of Labarde to which Cantenac should be linked, as Cantenac is only half a mile away, whereas, by the shortest route, it is two miles from Margaux;

"Seeing that the commune of Cantenac pleads the scandalous misuse of the name of Margaux as a pretext to ask that this misuse be, as it were, officially sanctioned by the addition of the name of Cantenac to that of Margaux;

"Seeing that names of communes are like those of families in that essentially they have an individuality to be respected; that it cannot be denied that the individuality of this name brings a certain advantage to property buyers reflected in the prices they pay; that to share the commercial value of the name of Margaux with a neighbouring commune, however honourable this name may already be, would harm the proprietors of Margaux;

"Seeing that there would be no valid reason to refuse a similar demand presented by the communes of Arsac and Soussans contiguous with that of Margaux, that the station sign at Margaux should then read Margaux-Cantenac-Soussans-Arsac, which illustrates out of hand, by this unprecedented exception to the rule, how ridiculous such an innovation would be..."

Without making further comment on this savoury document in its original éclat, I observe that it contains a large number of the arguments used in the "Margaux trials", which lasted more than half a century. And, finally, that the huge Margaux family was enlarged to include the five communes mentioned. As if, without really being on the right rails, the Médoc railways contributed perhaps more than the post office to the present unification of the Margaux vineyards. But Margaux station is still called Margaux and its goods-train shed is rented today by a case-maker to store his orders from local châteaux owners who duly have the cases filled with their bottles and re-despatched by road to their faithful clients. What a long way we have come from the epic struggles on the No 26 country road between Margaux and Soussans!

In 1942, Monsieur Lafforgue, an official from the Institut National des Appellations d'Origine (INAO), made a detailed report. He concluded that the claims of Margaux and Cantenac to benefit from the Margaux appellation were acceptable but excluded Arsac and Labarde from benefiting from it. As far as Soussans was concerned, he hid behind the "case already heard" and did not pursue this any further. So the Margaux proprietors harvesting in Soussans were deprived of a considerable quantity of "Margaux wine".

Ten troubled years rolled by.

The INAO was to settle the question: Soussans would remain excluded. Cantenac, Arsac and Labarde would be admitted. Paul Zuger, the then president of the Association of Margaux Proprietors for the Protection and Defence of the Name of Margaux, himself a proprietor in the area of Marsac in Soussans, one of the best in the region – where Château Margaux and other *grands crus* also harvest

– was outraged and wrote a sour letter. In it he complained bitterly to the director of the INAO: "It would be heresy, a scandal, and totally illogical to give the Margaux AOC to properties situated four to five miles from Margaux proper, while the vineyards adjacent to Soussans-Marsac are condemned to be deprived of this appellation despite long-standing established practice and claims certainly as valid as those invoked by Labarde and Arsac. This has nothing to do with any legal claim for indeed, the judgements and decrees are the result of a tortuous procedure, ill-conceived, outdated and absurd."

A weighty argument was to fall onto the scales and tip them decisively. The Bordeaux trade providentially indicated that to make the name of Margaux commercially viable as an *appellation d'origine*, they would need sufficient quantities, which could not be provided without the help of the good land round the Margaux region.

This is how August 10, 1954 came about, a date which I have already mentioned.

▲ *Viticulture generates a number of related commercial and industrial activities. Today, the majority are centred round mechanical agricultural equipment. At Margaux, the case-maker, Robert Bergey, makes the traditional "caisses de 12" which supply all the* grands crus.

On January 20, 1683, Jean-Baptiste Colbert, the king's minister, concerned for the welfare of the kingdom, wrote to his intendant in Bordeaux: "These merchants may have more sense than the magistrates."

The art of a merchant is not only to know how to sell, but to know what he is buying. As far as wine goes, this knowledge is both indispensable and delicate. It is complex. And yet, it is that which counts. With château-bottling becoming more general, dictated by the twofold concern of the producer to protect his label and that of the consumer who thereby has a guarantee of authenticity, the merchants have become telex-senders and catalogue editors. They buy labels and they resell them. It is up to the "client" to sort it all out and to distinguish between the good and the bad, for, relatively speaking, there are always good and bad wines. A proprietor will never tell you his wine is bad. An adept merchant will avoid offering it to you, so endorsing the contract of confidence between himself and his customer. But third parties who operate like this have a difficult rôle they do not properly understand. As far as Margaux is concerned, like the majority of the great Bordeaux appellations, I will say that it is the Bordeaux wine trade which has created, maintained and developed the fame of the wines. Certainly, they knew what land they were building on. But that is the whole point: they *knew...*

"It is known that all the wines taken on from Bordeaux are not wines from Grave and that there are infinitely more which come from Palus – low land with rich soil, giving rich firm wines, so much sought after by people from the North. It is up to the buyers to take them for what they are, after tasting them, without basing themselves on the pompous titles given them by the merchants. For these merchants are Gascons, and just like the Italians, enjoy the privilege of exaggerating whatever they say as much as they want. None the less, it must be observed that when these Palus wines have been well chosen and have travelled at sea, they improve and are infinitely better in the dependencies than in the country of their origin" (*Nouveau Voyage aux Isles de l'Amérique*, Paris, 1722).

This distinction between the Graves wines and the Palus wines is the basis for distinguishing the differences among the Bordeaux vineyards. Towards the beginning of the eighteenth century, the idea of "Côtes wines" was wisely included. But here it is essential to understand that the term "Graves wines" covered the whole of the *crus* situated on the gravel terraces, that is to say principally the present vine-growing region of Graves, to the south west of Bordeaux, and the whole of the Upper Médoc as far as Saint-Estèphe. So, for a wine lover of 1750, "Grave" meant all the gravelly terrain on the left bank of the Garonne and the Gironde. It is the urbanization of Bordeaux encroaching onto the surrounding vine-growing land which has split this geological reality in two, the southern part retaining the name "Graves" and the northern part becoming the "Médoc". But previously, it was the plains of the Médoc and the extreme point of the peninsula which were called "Médoc" (*in medio aquae*), "that lonely, wild country" as La Boétie called it.

In short, in the eighteenth century, the wine of Margaux was well and truly Graves wine. We can be quite convinced of this by reading *Mémoire sur le commerce de Bordeaux* published in 1730: "There are five principal *crus* in the seneschalsy of Bordeaux called Graves, Palus, Entre-deux-Mers, Langon, Barsac and Preignac. Each of these *crus* can be subdivided further into different types according to the different prices commanded by the wines they produce:

"The Graves wine is both red and white. The red breaks down into three main types. The first includes the *crus* Pontac, Lafitte and Château de Margo, which generally produce only three hundred tonneaux of wine, which is the most highly rated in the whole province and which generally sells at 1,200 to 1,500 livres per tonneau. The majority of this wine is exported to England.

"The second includes an infinite number of *crus* which it is impossible to list. The wines they produce are sold in an average year at 300 to 500 livres per tonneau, and they are exported to England, Ireland, Scotland, Holland and Hamburg.

"The third produces wines whose price generally speaking ranges from 100 to 200 livres per tonneau. Among these, the cheapest are consumed in Brittany, Normandy, Picardy and Dunkirk and the dearest in the department of the Nord.

"White Graves wine generally sells at 100 to 200 livres per tonneau and goes to England, Holland, Flanders and Paris." More than a century before the classification of the great wines of the Médoc and Sauternes, a clear hierarchy existed. The *Mémoire* of 1730 does not enumerate the "infinite number of *crus* which it is impossible to list"; but the variations in the prices paid at the time reveal the differences in quality, going hand in hand with the different places where the wine was consumed, the best naturally going to the richest. To mention only the "Graves wines", the price range of 100 to 1,500 is the same today in more or less equivalent proportions. That is what I call the regional premium.

Centuries of experiments and observations were needed to arrive at this point. It is not by chance that Margaux is at the top of the pyramid today. A set of preliminary conditions existed at the very start. They were the result of the combination of four essential elements: soil, subsoil, drainage and climate. Their existence stimulated people seeking perfection, leading them finally to the profound

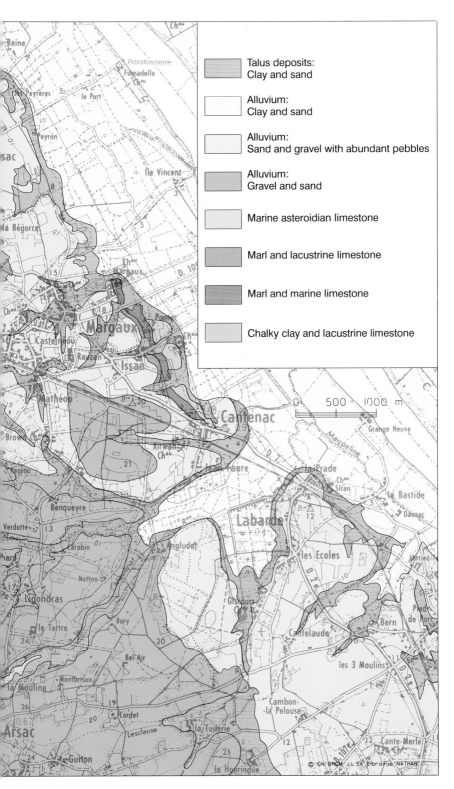

Talus deposits:
Clay and sand

Alluvium:
Clay and sand

Alluvium:
Sand and gravel with abundant pebbles

Alluvium:
Gravel and sand

Marine asteroidian limestone

Marl and lacustrine limestone

Marl and marine limestone

Chalky clay and lacustrine limestone

0   500   1000   m

© IGN BRGM J.L.SA Librairie NATHAN

knowledge they now possess. Progress in the use of different grape varieties, cultivation and vinification has been grafted onto the conditions provided initially by nature which had already brought together elements rarely found in any one place.

"The terrain of the Margaux appellation which takes in Arsac, Soussans, Margaux, Cantenac and Labarde, has gravelly soil, which is the first requirement in the Médoc for viticultural agrology, and the extraordinary way in which the network of the brooklets of Le Moulinat has cut through the gravels has provided an excellent example of ridges. We could almost say that at the cost of losing a good quarter of its size of vineyard which has been transformed into marshland, the Margaux appellation has, for the sake of its vines, afforded itself the luxury of an archipelago of hills and slopes which are without equivalent in the Bordeaux region." This observation by Professor Henri Enjalbert, made with regard to Château Giscours, is in my opinion the best explanation for the individuality of the Margaux vineyards. A simple glance at a map of the vineyards in the appellation reveals the reality of this archipelago which I am personally tempted to compare to the flagship of a fleet – an aircraft carrier whose prow is Marsac, whose stern Cantenac, and whose bridge, Château Margaux, is set to the starboard side; it is surrounded by seven other vessels which escort it. Whichever of these two similes you choose, the principal idea not to lose sight of is the land masses emerging above the surrounding marshlands, this being the very guarantee of perfect natural drainage. Without going into the complexity of agricultural science, I will say that the vine is a sort of still which distils water. In Margaux, the soil is siliceous (pebbles and gravel), and so is highly permeable and extremely poor, but rich in oxides and mineral salts. Over the seasons, the level of the water-table varies. There is a more abundant water supply at the beginning of the agricultural year, which favours the development of the vegetation, but which gradually reduces as maturity takes place. In order to have the best conditions for the still to function correctly, a regular water supply and plenty of sunshine are necessary. Since the latter is synonymous with drought, it is the old vines, whose roots penetrate deepest (down to 15 or 18 feet), which keep the action of the still going most effectively, but even so, often at the expense of the yield of grapes. The average age of a vineyard is important as regards quality. At least seven years are needed for a vine to pro-

Today, the tractor drivers are accustomed to the narrow rows and low-lying vines of the Médoc. But they still have to be very careful, especially on entering and leaving the vineyards.

duce normally and nearly fifteen before it attains its best yield. This is the experience of centuries. The strength that comes with maturity is found in a vineyard of thirty to fifty years old, and even older if the harvest is to reach the very peak of quality. The great estates are privileged, for they can renew their plants slowly and the great growers are those who, discounting short-term profit and yield (that demon whose demands enslave so many), plan patiently and prudently when to uproot and when to replant.

For a long time, the average yield per hectare in the Margaux *crus classés* was less than 30 hectolitres. A general improvement in viticultural agronomy has progressively increased this average to 40 to 45 hectolitres. I think this is a limit not to be exceeded. "So, when I see such and such a famous appellation ask the INAO for authorization to produce 70 hectolitres per hectare... I really think this is suicide" (Bernard Ginestet, *La Bouillie bordelaise,* Paris, 1975).

In this respect, Margaux remains one of the most reasonable of the great appellations of the Médoc, of the whole of Bordeaux, of France, Navarre and the whole world.

And yet, is this proportion not dictated by nature? For Margaux can doubtless claim to have the "poorest" viticultural land of all the Bordeaux area. There is abundant gravel but there is a great dearth of humus and vegetable matter. It would be possible to rectify this deficiency with fertilizer. Certain *crus* do not fail to do so but there is an immediate decline in quality. For young plants, the best compost in the world is, by preference, manure. When the roots are sufficiently deep, the vine plant can be callously allowed to suffer malnutrition in organic compounds for this asceticism is the price it has to pay in order to attain the mystical perfection of the *chef d'œuvre.*

The slopes and gravel terraces of the Margaux appellation are, in the geological sense, recent alluvial deposits. They date only from the period known as Pleistocene, in the early part of the Quaternary era. Over a period of only 8,000 centuries, and rarely more than once each century, the Garonne swept down in a huge flood, tumbling, washing, polishing and depositing a vast quantity of pebbles and stones carried down from the Pyrenees or the southern Massif Central. (One further feature which distinguishes Margaux from the other Médoc appellations further downstream – Saint-Julien, Pauillac, Saint-Estèphe – is that its terrain is composed of a higher proportion of gravel from the Pyrenees and Garonne, whereas the others are composed in the main of material from the Dordogne.) This long and turbulent journey had the effect of sorting out the strong, resistant material from the more fragile (limestone, granite, etc.) which was unable to survive the conditions in the torrent.

So there remains a splendid selection of mineralogies, some volcanic, some sedimentary, of all shapes and sizes, rather like a fruit salad of pebbles. In the main, this multicoloured mixture of stones is quartz, milky, glassy or bluish, depending on the metallic oxides present during crystallization. There is grey and pink quartzite, Jurassic flint, layered agates veined like luxury marbles which children play with, green sandstone often striped with quartz veins, black
46 and white chert which looks really prehistoric, lydians or phthanites

going through every shade of grey, green, brown or black... The Count of Hargicourt, who was the lord of Margaux towards the end of the eighteenth century some years before the storming of the Bastille, appeared one day at the court of Louis XVI wearing a coat whose buttons gleamed like diamonds. The courtiers' whisperings were so unrestrained that the king's attention was drawn to his colonel's luxurious apparel. "But Sir, you must be the wealthiest man in the kingdom!" Hargicourt flushed scarlet and declared: "Sire, I am just wearing the diamonds from my own estate!"

Following a practice now abandoned, the Count of Hargicourt had had rock crystals gathered from his vineyards cut and polished, so that they gleamed like imitation diamonds. (*Encycl.:* "Paste jewellery makes use of stones from the Médoc, the Rhine, Bristol, which are variously coloured rock crystal, as well as pebbles from Cayenne and Alençon, which are varieties of quartz.")

The same story has also been told but with a change of personalities: the Marquis de Ségur and Louis XV. In this version, the stones came from Château Latour. But the Marchioness Aguado de Las Marismas, who knew that the story originated from "her" land in Margaux, used to ask the vignerons' children to find her these diamond-like pebbles for which she paid, so the nineteenth century story goes, as if they were genuine diamonds. It appears that this gave the gracious marchioness tremendous notoriety in the region. After her, no one else carried on this type of patronage, but "diamonds" are still to be found at the foot of the cabernet-sauvignon in Margaux.

But apart from their suitability for adorning princes, apart from allowing air and water access to the vines' roots, and apart from their striking poverty, the gravel and pebbles of the Médoc have one more virtue: that of acting as heat regulators. Not only do they act as tiny mirrors, reflecting the sun's rays towards the bunches of grapes, ensuring steady ripening, but they also absorb the heat the sun has given out all through the day and reflect it back to the grapes during the night. That is why the supports holding the vine-branches are kept at the lowest possible level. In this way, the harvest is close to its heat source. And that is also why local grape pickers cannot work upright. For a low-growing vine is not a whim of nature. It is even against its own inclination to grow without climbing. For, just like wistaria, it would prefer to climb up its support however high it is. (Egyptian paintings depict grape pickers reaching high into the air. Roman slaves who were put to picking climbing vines were at high risk, for there were many who fell and broke a limb.) The cabernet and its recent cousin the cabernet-sauvignon are particularly suited to gravelly soils. It is the art of the grower to contain the growth, 47 keeping it low down. As long ago as 1845 Count Odart said "At least that is how it is done in the Médoc."

Montesquieu called it "the hardy little vine grown on gravelly soils". Depending on the regions, it can be called *breton, véronais, arrouya*. In Bordeaux, it is also called *carmenet, carmenère, bidure, vidure* or *petite-vuidure*. Several reliable authors are in agreement and see it as the *vitis biturica*, otherwise called the Bordeaux vine, today so widely spread over the vine-growing area of western France. This is how Count Odart describes it: "It is easy to recognize from its thin slender leaves, with their five smooth rounded lobes – that is to say that they have no down or pubescence on their underside; also from their bunches giving but few grapes of average size, round, tight-clustered, very black and with a distinctive flavour; from its stalk and wine-coloured (dark violet) pedicles, and in winter from the colour of the bark of its long branches – light red tending to fawn. The wine it produces is elegant, subtle, full of bouquet, light in colour and can be kept for a long time. All these good qualities vary slightly according to the nature of the soil." At Margaux, these good qualities are multiplied tenfold. We can rightly say that it is the perfect marriage between the vine and its soil. The *petit-cabernet* or cabernet-sauvignon at Margaux in the Médoc is what the *coffea arabica* is to Blue Mountain in Jamaica. The time when it was first planted and adapted goes back to the Gallo-Roman period, and, in the strict sense of the term, we can say that it "took root", so much so that the Bordeaux people of the earliest times, the Bituriges Vivisques, gave their name to it. At the very beginning of the seventh century, Archbishop Isidore de Séville, speaking of vines and wines, mentions that "the strain called Biturique takes its name from the land where it is grown. It strenuously resists storms, rain and heat and even thrives in poor soil. In this respect, it is better than all the others." Ten centuries later, Cardinal de Richelieu, learning of the qualities of the petit-cabernet, uprooted several thousand from the best Graves area of Bordeaux (to which Margaux belonged at that time) to send them to his intendant, the priest breton, who spread this form of evangelism dictated by his superior so widely that, under the new name of "breton", this variety conquered all the west of France and particularly the Loire region.

Although the cabernet is the basic variety for vineyards in Margaux, it is not the only one. By contrast, the merlot gives a range of complementary qualities: colour, richness in alcohol and softness. It

---

Pebbles from Margaux which have simply been polished with an abrasive powder.
Some of them could be faceted in Antwerp to be made into attractive necklaces. ▶

is less resistant than the cabernet-sauvignon and it ripens quicker. It is rarely to be found in large proportions in Margaux, but it is a very valuable back-up variety. It grows best in well-drained land and is extremely sensitive to grey rot. So it has to be harvested without delay as soon as it has reached maturity. The respective times the merlots and cabernets reach full maturity allow the grower to harvest to a convenient rhythm. In the great years, the merlot gives an exceptional rounded warmth which combines perfectly with the vigour and finesse of the cabernet. It is probably because of its high sugar content that thrushes and blackbirds are particularly fond of it. It is even said that it takes its name from the blackbird ("merle" in French). It first appeared in Margaux at the beginning of the nineteenth century.

Apart from the cabernets and merlots, Margaux has two other different grape varieties: the malbec (or malbeck) and the petit-verdot. The first spread in the Médoc at the beginning of the eighteenth century. It is said to have been "imported" from Cahors by Monsieur Malbeck in person. It is a variety which is well adapted to rich soil and limestone. This is why it is mainly found in the commune of Soussans, where the limestone substratum is not too far down. The small growers are generally much attached to the malbecs which ensure both robustness and rapid maturity. Malbec wines throw their lees rapidly. They are delicate with a clearly pronounced, characteristic bouquet. In a large vineyard, the principal problem is that the variety is difficult to prune. It needs all the loving, constant and faithful skill of the vigneron, who knows each of his plants individually, to be able to be successful with a parcel of land planted with malbecs.

As for the petit-verdot, its very name indicates its verdant green colour. It is a variety whose grapes ripen late but which gives the necessary vigour to ensure the sturdiness of the wine as it ages, thanks to a good fixed acidity. In the eighteenth century, trade with the dependencies flourished. Tonneaux of great wine were exported by sea in the thousands. Wines which were sufficiently robust were essential. The petit-verdot gave the **dot**al – dowry – part of its name to help. It became indispensable to mitigate the extreme delicacy of the cabernet reinforcing it with its vigour, which can sometimes be rather biting. Curiously enough, the verdots are among the first to flower and the last to ripen. In Margaux, they are used in small proportions and in certain cold, wet years, their grapes are not used for the great wines. If the merlot is the unctuous complement of the cabernet, the verdot gives the bite and an inimitable perfume of violet. Originally a variety from the loamy soils, the verdot gained a foothold on the

Médoc's slopes and slowly and imperceptibly assumed an increasingly important rôle, ensuring that the great wines' journeys by sea should not destroy their essential character or virtues. This having been said, it should be mentioned that wine made out of pure verdots is difficult to drink alone. There need to be several people, at least four: one to drink and three to hold the drinker up. An old sorcerer from Virefougasse used to claim that it was a powerful diuretic. Whatever the case, if you will pardon my sudden vulgarity, Margaux wine can be as easily peed as drunk, with or without verdot. It is a property which is always overlooked in sales publicity.

Here I should speak of the variety introduced since the great phylloxera crisis at the end of the nineteenth century. I will simply say that ampelography, or the science of grape varieties, has made considerable progress within a hundred years. The way the variety adapts to the soil, the subsoil and to the nature of the drainage and the microclimate is an important factor in the success of any young plant. The nurserymen supply sets to order, which are grafted according to the needs of the grower. The majority come from the region of Blaye or Saint-Emilion, where the land favours this type of production. Several *crus* have used direct grafting. The variety is first planted and once it has struck root, it is grafted on the spot onto the premium variety. It was my father, Pierre Ginestet, who introduced this practice at Margaux towards the end of the thirties. At that time, he was also proprietor of Château Rabaud-Promis in Sauternes, where this procedure was current practice. But it was completely unknown in the Médoc and people did not know how to go about it. He brought his superintendent from Rabaud to Château Margaux, along with a team of Sauternes vignerons who thus became the pioneers of a new viticultural technique in the Médoc. Although this method, which in point of fact is rather costly, offers many advantages, there are very few vignerons today able to carry out grafting directly onto the vine.

At Château Margaux, the last parcel of cabernet-franc vines, not grafted, dating from about 1870, was uprooted in 1983. They were a witness to the past. To my knowledge, the little plot called the "Orangery" was the only portion of French vines in the Médoc which resisted the phylloxera. But time took its toll. Yet they used to reproduce by layering and might today have been able to carry on their

---

This photograph, taken from the water-tower in Margaux, shows several parcels of vines with the church in the middle. Behind, we see the river and, on the horizon, the Côtes de Bourg on the opposite bank. ▶

century-old loyal service. Out of all the Margaux appellation, the oldest vines still in production could well be those of René Renon, in Marsac, which were planted in his great-grandfather's time.

Just as everywhere else, the four main stages in the agricultural year up to picking are pruning, budding, flowering and the *véraison*, that is, the moment the grapes start to take colour. As far as pruning is concerned, some people advocate that it should be done as soon as possible after the leaves fall. Others prefer to wait until the first frosts have occurred. There is an old adage which I have heard quoted many and many a time: "Prune in the spring, prune in the fall-Pruning in March is best of all." This recommendation is good for all small vineyards, but the great estates stagger their pruning right through the winter and, depending on the years, the saying is proved or disproved.

Budding is when the vine puts forth its first leaves, followed by the "mannes", the embryos of the grapes, which give a fair indication of the size of the future harvest. It is also the critical time of the spring frosts which, within the space of one hour of intense cold, can cause considerable damage.

The majority of the *grands crus* fight these frosts with artificial smoke... much to the disapproval of road users. The notorious "Icy Saints" whose festival is on 11, 12, 13 May, Saint Mamert, Saint Pancrace and Saint Servais (people also include Saint Gervais, but wrongly so, for his festival was on 19 June in the old calendar), are the three angels of the viticultural apocalypse.

But we cannot halt progress. Since the calendar was corrected by Pope Gregory XIII and his Jesuit mathematicians, it is Saint Estelle, Saint Achille and Joan of Arc who have turned frigid. And no one any longer has the right to invoke Saint Pancrace to soothe away chilblains. But since the "Icy Saints" have been knocked off their pedestals, the average May temperature has shown itself milder towards the growers and the May moon less baleful. In France, mid-May is generally "hot".

The flowering, which takes place towards the end of May or at the beginning of June is the real harbinger of the forthcoming harvest, at least as far as quantity is concerned. Observation over the years shows that the maturing of the grapes will take place one hundred days after the flowering (some say a hundred and ten or a hundred and fifteen after the very first flower appears, which comes to more or less the same thing). The average date of the flowering should be noted to work out the calculation. Sometimes, it is difficult to know what the average date is. At Margaux (is it by chance?), it takes place on the same day as the flowering of the first lily. The kitchen gardener at Château Margaux has always kept a few lilies in order to note down in his diary the beginning of the hundred days countdown. And it works! The risk of frosts is no more to be feared.

It is now, however, that the spectre of Scylla appears: *coulure,* a faulty cross-pollination of the flower for whatever reason (degeneration, parasites, disease or, more often than not, bad weather). *Coulure* is also called *millerandage.* The result is that the future grapes remain at the foetal stage and do not develop. At the end of September, they are still very small, hard and unripe. Sometimes *coulure* has the effect of a good purgative blood-letting, if the harvest is too abundant. In this case, it is nature correcting itself, for the plants which are too heavily laden are at pains to see their large family reach maturity. In a normal year, *coulure* can represent a considerable loss in quantity. I will tell you a secret: the chestnut trees flower two or three weeks before the vines. If their flowers are not properly pollinated, which (unlike the flower of the vines) can be seen by the naked eye, you can play at being a fortune-teller and announce to your neighbouring proprietor: "We shall be suffering from *coulure* this year." If such is not the case, you had best forget your prediction.

Fifty days after the flowering, that is halfway between blossoming and maturity, there is the colour change. The grapes begin to take colour and their skin becomes slightly translucent. The old vignerons call this metamorphosis the "change". A lot has gone on since April. We are now in August. The personality of the future infant is soon to be determined. A country saying has captured this process rather neatly: "June makes the wine – July the bouquet – August makes the must" (some say "the flavour").

The unique flavour of the wine of Margaux is incomparable; it comes from its discreet complexity. The wines of other terrains can be identified by pronounced characteristics. This pleases people, for they are more easily identifiable – like an individual who has thick lips or a huge nose. Margaux wine is a perfect balance. In point of fact, you need a fine palate to be able to appreciate its perfumes and flavours and its mysterious effects on the senses. There is no violence or aggressiveness whatever. An exquisite charm arising from

On arrival, the harvest is tipped into a hopper. After the removal of the stalks, the grapes are lightly crushed and the pulp and juice are pumped into the fermentation vats (as here, at Château Monbrison). ▶

supreme distinction. A bouquet which is both floral and fruity. Such "a chord" as charms by its harmony. In the cold, wet years, its delicacy can turn to fragility, but even in its slenderness, it will still remain an aristocrat. In the great years, it is a sovereign.

As regards the soil of the five communes of the Margaux appellation, I have quoted Charles Cocks who, in 1850, plagiarized William Franck, writing: "Margaux wines are extremely subtle, have a fine colour and a very suave bouquet which fills the mouth; they are generous without being heady, they quicken the stomach yet respect the head and leave the breath unsullied and the mouth fresh." Franck had already said the very same thing some few years earlier almost word for word. It should not be considered that Cocks's plagiarizing this appraisal was an easy way out; it simply confirmed the general reputation enjoyed by Margaux wines in the nineteenth century.

This description is today published in almost every work which speaks of Margaux. Some quote it verbatim, like a well-learned catechism and no one would dream for a moment of applying it other than to Margaux wines. That is how history is written and comes to be printed. Yet I have tracked this epic phrase back to its source which is *La Topographie de tous les vignobles connus,* published in 1816 by A. Jullien. The author comments on "the wines of Bordeaux which are too well known for any eulogy to be able to enhance their reputation... When a Bordeaux wine of first quality has come to its full maturity, it should be extremely subtle, have a fine colour, a very suave bouquet and a savour which fills the mouth. It should be powerful without being heady and have body without being bitter; it should quicken the stomach yet respect the head, leaving the breath unsullied and the mouth fresh. If these wines are kept unadulterated, they can be drunk in large quantities without any disagreeable effects." So then, that is the key to the mystery. But is it likely that Margaux wines could have thrived on the reputation of those of Bordeaux for one-and-a-half centuries? This is unlikely. In fact, a close study reveals that Franck, Cocks and the others found Jullien's eulogy excessive, being unreservedly addressed to all Bordeaux wines. They deliberately used it to apply to Margaux wines only, considering that the zeal of their predecessor could have been due only to absorbing "in large quantities" a variety of Margaux wines!

Today's president of the Viticultural Federation of the Margaux Appellation, Monsieur Roger Zuger, goes into detail concerning variety: "If the wines of Margaux resemble one another by their body, there is a wealth and variety of *bouquets,* and of fruity flavours which are different from one château to another. With these, too, the structure of the land is different. Certain properties have a higher gravel

VIN DE MARGAUX

Le Premier Vin du Monde ═══
Véritable élixir de longue Vie

Le Vin de Margaux ranime l'estomac sans fatiguer la tête. L'haleine reste pure et la bouche fraîche, car il a beaucoup de force sans être fumeux. Sa couleur est splendide et il a un bouquet incomparable.

Il est surtout caractérisé par une suprême finesse de goût, qui lui donne une distinction sans égale.

 Acheter du MARGAUX...
═══ c'est acheter ═══
de la JOIE et de la SANTÉ

or sand content, others have drier or damper soil... it is the total of these individual qualities which makes up the variety and richness of Margaux wines."

It is true that the variety is great for such a restricted area. Each gravel slope has its own personality with its different exposures and microclimates. The whole of the appellation covers approximately 1,000 hectares. Before it existed in its official form, the area producing Margaux wines was much larger, partly because of improper use of the name by neighbouring areas. But then the crisis of the thirties reduced the size of vineyard. All the good wine-producing land was not taken into consideration at the time of the confirmation of the Margaux AOC. The best example is Château d'Arsac which is still, as it were, in the "purgatory" of the "Haut-Médoc AOC" whereas it could justifiably claim the rank of a Margaux *cru bourgeois*. The area of Virefougasse in Soussans is in my opinion wrongly cut off from Margaux by the departmental road from Margaux to Castelnau. On the southern limits of Arsac, there are the stretches of Médoc flatlands which predominate, intersected by gravel-pits or quarries for extracting gravel. A prefectoral ruling has recently put a curb on the appetite of the makers of cement. The time had come to preserve these reserves of gravel which, if developed with a drainage network

▲ A prospectus published in the thirties by the Viticultural Federation of Margaux, convincingly extolling the properties of its wines.

of canals, could produce very good wine. Other similar cases exist. Obviously they are all difficult to judge, especially when compared with firmly established situations.

In relation to the Land Register of 1855, the date of the official classification of the *crus* of the Médoc, it is certain that the great estates were privileged, their vineyards under production being globally incorporated into the appellation, whereas many small growers owning neighbouring parcels were refused the appellation. A few rare extensions have taken place. A serious revision of the Margaux AOC would seem to me desirable, as well as a sound lesson at the same time on the tenuous use of this name by people who are not even on the boundary of the commune! But that is how it is! Every dog has its fleas!

Out of the fifty-seven *crus classés* in the Médoc (Haut-Brion apart), spread over the appellations of Margaux, Saint-Julien, Saint-Estèphe, Pauillac and Haut-Médoc, twenty-two are in the Margaux AOC, with one distinguishing feature, namely that every division in the classification is represented, from the first to the fifth.

I must mention that the names of the *crus* listed here correspond to the correct names (Malescot Saint-Exupéry instead of Saint-Exupéry;

▲ *This waste land is at Arsac where many waterlogged gravel quarries mottle the once-green countryside. The relief of the slopes has been perforated by the gravel diggers. The cabernets and merlots will never find a home here again.*

Marquis d'Alesme-Becker rather than Becker; Prieuré-Lichine instead of Le Prieuré...) and that on the the other hand, Pouget-Lassalle and Pouget have been merged into the one name of Château Pouget.

This list is incomparable. It is like a train drawn by a famous engine – the famous Château Margaux – and even the fifth class carriages are extremely luxurious.

Apart from the *grands crus classés,* there are a good fifty other châteaux in Margaux, from the most modest "artisan" to the "bourgeois supérieur", even "bourgeois exceptionnel". The term "cru bourgeois" has never convinced me. Some regard it nostalgically as an aristocratic rank which they have never been able to attain. They form themselves into a sort of Third Estate. The artificial distinction between *cru classé* and *cru bourgeois* seems very harsh to me. As proof, I can think of the many blind tastings in which modest "petits bourgeois" have been taken for great wines (and vice versa). That is why I will say that, if the 1855 classification has the enormous virtue of existing, a true wine lover would not let himself fall into the error of being its slave. The appreciation of taste should not let itself be manipulated in this way. Out of the thirty-five or so *crus bourgeois* 61 in Margaux, you can discover sumptuous wines which, apart from leaving your breath unsullied and your mouth fresh, will leave you with pleasant memories and a desire to drink them again... and this is true right down to the meanest: for example, the wine of Francis Moizeau, a blacksmith in Margaux, which is, believe you me, the most difficult wine of all to find.

The "small growers" – that is, those who have, say, less than five hectares of vines – are becoming increasingly rare in Margaux. The exodus from country to town stemmed mainly from the families of artisan vignerons. The great estates, on the contrary, helped to stabilize employment. These latter gobbled up, parcel by parcel, the micro-productions which today represent no more than 10% of the appellation. Certain *crus classés* have followed a systematic policy of reorganization, either to reconstitute their estates, split up over the generations, within the limits of the 1855 Land Register, or quite simply to increase their production, sometimes in impressive proportions. Here for example is the evolution of the amounts harvested at Château Lascombes in the second half of the last century:

> 1850: 15 tonneaux
> 1868: from 16 to 20 tonneaux
> 1874: 25 tonneaux
> 1886: 35 tonneaux

In Féret's twelfth edition of *Bordeaux et ses vins* (1969), we read: "Since the acquisition of this property by Monsieur Lichine and his financial group, in the spring of 1952, the wines produced by Lascombes have become the most sought after and respected on the Anglo-Saxon market and particularly in the United States, where Château Lascombes acts as an ambassador for French wines. After several purchases of land made by Monsieur Lichine and the regrouping of various parcels of land, the property consists of 88 hectares, enabling it to produce 200 to 270 tonneaux."

The predilection of the Anglo-Saxons has become so strong that since 1971, the British group, Bass-Charrington has presided over the destiny of Lascombes. The property has 94 hectares of vines and declares an annual production of 400,000 to 500,000 bottles, that is, an average of nearly 400 tonneaux or a yield of about 40 hectolitres per hectare (which, nominally, is reasonable). This inflation, in the order of 1,200% over 30 years must be a record. As we are not dealing with paper money, it is quite clear that the source of this increase must have come from somewhere within the Margaux appellation.

In 1850, Charles Cocks listed 13 producers in Labarde, 18 in Cantenac, 19 in Arsac, 19 in Soussans and 43 at Margaux, that is a total of 112.

In 1922, the number of people registering harvest return figures in the five communes was more than 170 (at that time, unfortunately, it was difficult to know exactly what was harvested on the "graves" and what came from the "palus").

In 1949, Cocks and Féret listed:
- 38 proprietors in Arsac, of whom some 30 produce from 1 to 5 tonneaux;
- 30 proprietors in Labarde, of whom some 20 produce from 1 to 3 tonneaux;
- 58 proprietors in Cantenac, of whom some 20 produce from 1 to 3 tonneaux;
- 36 proprietors at Margaux, of whom some 10 or so produce from 1 to 5 tonneaux;
- 44 proprietors in Soussans, of whom some 20 produce from 1 to 5 tonneaux;

that is a total of 206 growers, of whom half were very small producers (account was not taken of the wines from the "palus").

Forty years later, the cards have been dealt anew. The *crus classés* and the best *bourgeois* have reshaped and increased their land surfaces according to their fame. And the Viticultural Federation of Margaux takes in some seventy-nine proprietors, about thirty of whom have less than three hectares.

This in itself indicates the considerable amount of land and estates, creating *ipso facto* a large number of names, and accordingly, labels. In my opinion, the degeneration of the Bordeaux wine trade since the last war has been a complementary and important factor in this development. In the great appellations, the name of the wine merchant or, if you prefer, his signature, is worth no more than that of the producer. There is practically no longer any "generic Margaux" to be found. As everyone stands shoulder to shoulder in this battle, financial ammunition has been channelled to the proprietors, thanks to special loans by the Crédit Agricole, to enable them to complete the indispensable ageing process themselves, as well as bottling and even marketing. At the same time, the best financially armed business-houses have counter-attacked by buying up important *crus* and vineyards, more often than not with foreign capital. The case of Château Lascombes is an example; and it is not the only one. In the same way, what has happened in the Margaux appellation is true of the other vine-growing regions. The proprietors or administrators of *crus classés* have engaged in a merciless battle for the possession of land over the course of the last generation. If in this area people enquired after the health of old Joseph Marsac who, at seventy-eight years of age, was still looking after his vines, it would be to judge his

staying power and to calculate the chances of eventually getting hold of his 2.65 hectares of malbec, knowing that his children were not going to continue working the land. As for the late Alexis Lichine, he was the champion of leasing vines, even if it meant remunerating his landlords with a handsome, carefully calculated payment, thus sharing out equitably the financial benefit accruing to his product thanks to his name on the label. Lucien Lurton, the Zugers, the Taris and *tutti quanti* set themselves the task of enlarging their circle of influence at the same time as the perimeter of their viticulture.

As a result of this policy, all the *grands crus* have reconstructed or enlarged their working buildings, cellars and vat-houses, developing the installations for vinification and increasing storage capacity.

▲ *At Soussans, Georges Rabi is the very last proprietor in the Margaux AOC to cultivate his vines with a horse. He has all the latest catalogues of mechanical equipment for use on vineyards, but he remains faithful to "Bella", who is gentle with his malbec!*

Today, the sum total of all the wine-making buildings in the Margaux AOC is perhaps the most remarkable in the world in respect of quality and quantity, diversity and density. The château builders of the eighteenth and nineteenth centuries have given place to the modern builders of wine temples wherein all is order, luxury, calm and propriety.

If the estates have in most cases changed in size, the concept of the *cru*, their distinctive product, has become more restricted, though not necessarily stricter. Many of the 1855 *crus classés* have greater areas in production than they had 130 years ago and this is a two-edged sword as far as the consumer is concerned. On the one hand, he becomes more anonymous, swallowed up in a greatly increased number of customers; on the other, he can find his way more easily through a limited range of products which are at least comparable, if not actually similar. Current methods of distribution together with modern advertising have encouraged the idea, which producers must try to respect, that the demands of anyone wanting 75 centilitres of bottled dreams must be met. In a different sphere of activity, today's fashion houses, and even the great chefs, use the techniques of the advertiser to convince the customer that they are "up to date". The achievements of these now well-established practices may be open to criticism; all the same, I sometimes regret that the wine business uses such old-fashioned sales methods when its production techniques are so modern. We sometimes seem not to be in the right century (like the man who insists on having exposed oak beams in his house, what I call the "imitation oak-beams syndrome"). To be the heirs of a past is good. To carry it forward into the present and hand it on to the future is good too. But it is towards the present and the future that we must point the consumer; he must not be left wallowing in the belief that we are still using age-old vats and jealously preserving the secret methods and traditions of our ancestors.

There is no doubt about it: with everything in its favour, the wine made today is better than that made one, two or four centuries ago. There are no bad years now; there are only vintages with different characteristics. The former general practice of prolonged maturing in the wood was a mistake which has now been rectified. Vitivinicultural techniques, with their aim of improving quality, are the customer's best guarantee. Margaux is in the forefront of progress. Let this be proclaimed!

Even as recently as fifty years ago, Margaux's wines had few outlets. Great Britain, Holland and France took the lion's share. Today, the distribution is much wider, the American market taking a dominant place among the export countries, and exports to England have decreased. I think Alexis Lichine by himself was the voice of Margaux in America. Exports to Switzerland should be noted; they represent a far from negligible proportion of the whole (see p. 69).

Every year more and more tourists come to visit the Margaux vineyards, principally from April to October, and especially at the time of harvesting. Many visit the *Maison du Vin* in Margaux, situated on the D.2 road, on the way out of the village as you come from Bordeaux. All the information for visiting the cellars is available there. Several *crus* leave a few cases of their recent vintages which can be bought on the spot. The Maison du Vin acts as an information bureau for the five communes of the Margaux appella-

A sign of the times: whole families of grape pickers can no longer be seen. On the horizon, engulfed in a sea of vines, the mechanical harvester can do the work of 40 cutters and porters. ▶

tion. It is run by the Viticultural Federation of the Margaux AOC, whose president is Monsieur Roger Zuger, who succeeded his father and displays the same zeal and devotion. Usually, when you want to visit a château, it is best to announce your intentions by telephone or have an itinerary drawn up by the hostesses in the Maison du Vin. Not all the châteaux have a full-time guide to show visitors round, and you will readily understand that if the cellar master is in the middle of racking his wine, he will not want to be disturbed by visitors. With the very small estates, it is best to make an appointment. Generally speaking, you will be well received. Note, however, that Margaux proprietors do not always have that warm and hearty joviality you find in other vine-growing regions. You will see very few of those home-made signs announcing "*dégustation-vente*", and if you want to taste wines in the cellars, take a loaf of fresh bread and a morsel of cheese, but not too soft or over-fermented. In fact, it is not common to indulge in on-site snacks, but you will be paid the honour of being treated like a professional.

As to gastronomy, things have developed of late. A few years ago, there was nothing. Today, without leaving the Margaux appellation, you can find four restaurants:

In Labarde: *L'Auberge des Grands Crus.* This is just after the little church with its attractive campanile. It occupies the little square

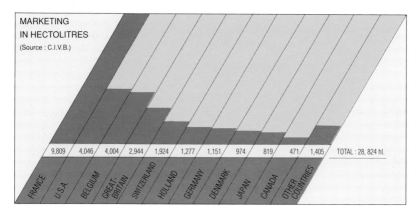

MARKETING
IN HECTOLITRES
(Source : C.I.V.B.)

FRANCE	U.S.A.	BELGIUM	GREAT-BRITAIN	SWITZERLAND	HOLLAND	GERMANY	DENMARK	JAPAN	CANADA	OTHER COUNTRIES	TOTAL : 28, 824 hl.
9,809	4,046	4,004	2,944	1,924	1,277	1,151	974	819	471	1,405	

on the farther side of the level crossing. The establishment is under new management and has now achieved a very respectable standard. There are ten or so modest bedrooms.

In Margaux itself: *L'Auberge de Savoie.* By the side of the Maison du Vin on the D.2, Monsieur and Madame Fougeras offer a sophisticated cuisine. The proprietor himself does the cooking and Madame does the front-of-house work. The menu is not a long litany of different dishes, but everything is perfectly prepared. Standing halfway between traditional French cooking and the *nouvelle cuisine,* Monsieur Fougeras lacks neither talent nor creativity. He is a true chef who rather prefers stews to roast and grilled meats served in their own natural juices. His little crayfish soufflés or snail vol-au-vents are excellent, as indeed are all his other inspired creations. The various meat dishes he prepares are appetizing, always hot and served with a selection of vegetables, always cooked to perfection (sometimes you may have to wait a little). There is a wide variety of delicious desserts, all home-made. The wine list is entirely comprehensive, obviously having a preponderance of *crus* from Margaux and the Médoc. This restaurant deserves a mention in the good food guides. The Fougerases have established a large and faithful clientele. You are advised to book in advance. The bill is perfectly reasonable and you get good value for your money, more so than in any big city.

Still in Margaux, today we have the *Relais de Margaux*, a splendid hotel belonging to the Relais de Campagne chain. As you leave the

◄ *The man in charge of the team keeps a close eye on the harvest as it is gathered. He extracts grapes which are insufficiently ripe and removes any leaves. Formerly, a preliminary crushing was carried out in the bin or half-butts on the vineyard. This practice has fortunately been discontinued for it gave rise to rapid oxidation.*

Margaux's Maison du Vin is the headquarters of the appellation's Viticultural Federation. It welcomes the numerous tourists who want to visit the châteaux. They can also buy a few bottles of the latest vintages here.   ►   69

village coming from Bordeaux, an impressive sign-board puts you on the right road. The Relais de Margaux has been built on the Domaine de l'Ile Vincent, close to Château Margaux by the river. Some thirty bedrooms have been equipped in perfect luxurious taste. Congress halls have all necessary audio-visual equipment. A tennis-court and swimming pool complete the outdoor facilities. After a halting start during the first four or five years, the cuisine is perfect thanks to the talented young chef, who has created an attractive menu at reasonable prices. Directed by the very competent Pierre Reymond, the Relais de Margaux has now found its rightful place among the top-class hotels of the region.

In Soussans: *Le Restaurant Larigaudière.* As you leave the village, you cannot fail to see on your left the entrance to Château Haut

Breton Larigaudière whose principal building, which has a bourgeois (like its *cru*) and opulent appearance, has just been restored.
The former chef of the restaurant known as Chez Philippe on the
Place du Parlement in the old quarter of Bordeaux has recently set
up here. Dominique Pradet was born seven miles or so from Larigaudière in the village of Moulis (where you can admire a splendid

---

▲ *Quality is a key-word at the Relais de Margaux, both in the hotel and in the
restaurant. The style of the cooking combines traditional "grande gastronomie" and
the more modern trends of nouvelle cuisine. (Phone: 56 88 38 30)*

◄ *In Margaux, Monsieur Fougeras is the ambassador of regional gastronomy. Though
young, he is a master of French cuisine. (Phone: 56 88 31 76)*   73

Romanesque church). At first, full of enthusiasm, he launched out into an over-elaborate cuisine, sometimes as complicated as the bills which followed. Local customers soon put him back on more traditional lines and now for quite a reasonable price, you can enjoy regional specialities such as snails, lamprey, game stew or *entrecôte,* salmi or the mushrooms known as "cèpes". If you ask, he will allow you to watch him at work in the kitchen. The restaurant is closed annually from November 15 to December 12. The gateway is impressive, you should not hesitate to go through it.

Local gastronomy is based simply on regional products, namely *entrecôte* steak and leg of lamb, shad and elvers, thrushes and *cèpe* mushrooms.

Entrecôte in the Margaux style is cooked exclusively over prunings of the cabernet vine, which should be at least several months old but not more than two years. The cut should be the thickness of two fingers (a vigneron's fingers, not those of a fairy) and should have a fair amount of fat. It is placed on a grill, already pre-heated, as soon

▲ *The attractive Larigaudière Restaurant is at Château Haut Breton Larigaudière in*
the village of Soussans. (Phone: 56 88 74 02)

as the flames die out. It should be seasoned with salt and freshly coarse-ground pepper along with a few good pinches of chopped shallots added when it is nearly cooked. Herbs, mustard and other exotic condiments should be dispensed with. It cuts very easily along the grain and should be accompanied by baked potatoes or three sizeable heads of *cèpe* mushrooms. You do not eat it, you savour it on a warm plate. It makes a perfect eternal marriage with Margaux wine – a young one or even one from your secret store.

Cèpes which come from Labarde, Arsac, Cantenac and Soussans are *premier cru cèpes* (for this product I will extend the appellation as far as Avensan and Le Pian). At Margaux itself, there are hardly any to be found, for there are no woods. The whole of the Médoc worships *cèpes*. Without being chauvinistic, I think that ours are the best. This is how Madame Germaine Grangerou, the wife of the late Marcel, one-time cellar master at Château Margaux (after his father Marcellus and before his own son Jean held this position)... this, then, is how she preserves *cèpes* which her husband gathered for her in places known only to him during the first quarter of the moon: "You place your *cèpes* on clean napkins on the kitchen table. Cut off the stalks and clean them, removing the earthy band at the end, and peel them delicately. Dry the top and underside of each head with a cloth. Then cover them with other cloths and leave them to dry out for a few hours (depending on how damp they are). Then you put them into a frying pan with a little very hot oil (just the barest amount) to drive out the remaining moisture, but for not more than three minutes either side. They should not be seasoned with anything. Then you place them in well-rinsed-out preserving jars and leave them to sterilize for two hours in a large basin of water. Leave them to cool slowly before storing the jars. The heads and stalks should have been put into separate jars. When the time comes to eat them, you will cook them in the normal way, just as if they had been freshly gathered: straight into hot oil with salt and pepper and, at the last minute, chopped garlic and parsley. And there you are." So that is how Madame Grangerou passes on to you one of our most precious culinary traditions. It appears easy. Try it, you will understand then. Even after two or three years in the jar, your *cèpes* will be just like those freshly gathered at first light. No deep-freeze is permitted in the true *cèpe* lovers' club!

Leg of mutton should come from Arsac by preference. But you could also get it from Pauillac or the Lower Médoc. It should not be too large (about five-and-a-half pounds in weight) and, if there are a lot of you, it is better to roast several smaller ones than one big one. You should ask the butcher to keep the nerve, that is to say, not to cut the tendon attached to the knuckle-bone. Light a good fire in the hearth with old cask staves, well encrusted with tartar*. When the fire has taken, about an hour before you sit down to table, hang the leg of lamb in front of the fire by a six-ply cord which has a wooden splint halfway down. The top of the cord should be attached to the under-side of the mantlepiece or from the chimney-hook if this hangs before the fire. The bottom of the leg should be some 6 inches away from the fire and 10 inches from a drip-pan placed directly beneath. This should be tilted towards you by means of a stone placed underneath it. You should twist the leg on its cord ten or so times. Then, just like an elastic spring, the cord will then rotate the leg and you have to do no more than watch it. From time to time, you will have to start the movement up again, but every time it comes to rest, you should carefully baste the leg with a mixture of vinegar, a little water, salt and pepper (and if you really must, add herbs and mustard). If the skin of the leg has been regularly basted, it will become crisp without burning. You must cut it at table and serve everybody as if you were the head of the family. The juice which has been collected in the drip-pan should be served separately in a very hot sauce-boat. With steamed green French beans, flageolets or haricot beans in a sauce; better still *cèpe* mushrooms, if you have any left. Success will be assured, especially if you put a satellite into orbit in the form of a magnum of Margaux of five to fifty-five years old. (If you do not have a magnum, get out three bottles; that will do, even if they are three different vintages within the age-range mentioned... the youngest to be served first.)

Shad is fished in the Garonne between the period of the vines coming into bud and their flowering. It can be caught between Macau and Soussans at the start of the ebb- or flow-tide and sometimes by moonlight – shades of Chateaubriand and Lamartine. It is a superb fish, belonging to the sardine family, but infinitely bigger than at Marseilles. You will need a "yawl" (a word which is very useful for Scrabble players). This is a kind of rowing-boat with an inboard mo-tor. You will also need a dragnet which should not exceed 150 feet if you are only a pleasure boater without a sea-fishing licence. The most difficult task is to disentangle it once it has been got back on board. Personally, I prefer spending an early morning fishing shad on the river with a close friend to all your shrimp fishing expeditions in Cabourg or anywhere else. Afterwards, it should be grilled on vine prunings whilst mother prepares a purée of sorrel, finely mashed. It's smashing, served with a dash of lemon! There is a special way of cutting the fish along the backbone to remove the maximum number

---

Over the years, the inner face of the oak staves which make up the casks becomes impregnated with tannin and wine deposits.

of bones. But there will always be some left. Its flesh is of the finest. A good little white Entre-deux-Mers wine is the order of the day but if you want to remain a partisan of Margaux, a *rosé* from Lascombes will be very appropriate or, rather more stylishly, a Pavillon Blanc from Château Margaux, the "white blackbird" of the red Médocs.

What are known locally and in Touraine as "pibales", but correctly termed elvers, are the fry of eels, caught in the channels near the river as from February. They are plentiful in the Gironde. They are exported to Spain where they fetch a high price and where, known as *angulas*, they are as much sought after as caviar. They are plunged alive, just as they are, into boiling oil. For barely one minute. They are drained, seasoned, served hot, or you can eat them cold with a vinaigrette. They are an acquired taste.

The thrush at harvest-time is one of the best small winged-game. It is said that a thrush devours three or four times its own weight in grapes every day. So just think of it! Thrushes stuffed with Margaux: what luxury! Traditionally, they are roasted on a spit over the fire or in the oven, stuffed with grapes. You can roll them in slices of bacon, but thrushes in October are as white and plump as the *filles de joie* of the Café de Paris in 1907. To cook them in the oven, just as grandmother used to do, there is an old recipe which involves making little individual containers out of parchment paper. Maybe, but there is a knack in folding it to make sure the juice is not lost. You can find how to do it in any handbook of Japanese origami. Otherwise, write to me and I will send you a sheet of white paper, and all you will have to do is to fold it.

Ever since I was born – at the foot of a cabernet-franc – I have heard and read a vast amount of rubbish about matching dishes with wines. A thirst for nonsensical refinement has taken hold of the would-be gourmets and several gastronomic journalists. Whatever else, Dodin Bouffant, Brillat-Savarin, Prosper Montagné and Curnonsky were clear and precise as to what they liked. Admittedly, they had refined tastes but not ridiculous ones. It is their literary style rising above the gastronomic pleasures they experienced which enables us to relive them still today. Great cuisine exists and I acknowledge it as a true art. If, when it comes to wine, tradition seems a reliable basis, then it should be followed right into the kitchen. Breast of duck with a purée of Spanish melon, veal liver with mint or sorrel, raw mignon of beef with tropical spices, vegetable omelette sprinkled with gravy might sometimes tempt your blasé appetite. In that case, you should modestly treat yourself to an appropriate wine made for the unexpected, the unsuited... and even the unfitting. On the other hand, it would not be fitting on your part to want to drink a real Margaux with a real chicken tandoori. In short,

there are values and flavours to be avoided. By and large, they are herbs, acidity, sweetness, the highly spiced, and the over-fermented. Apart from that, all Margaux wines go very well with all entrées, all meats, whether roasted or in stews, and any cheese you could put them to. This gives me the chance to observe that France and the French in general are slaves to wine at table and that there are other ways of savouring it. I know many well-to-do families in northern Europe, starting with Belgium, who after dining early, spend an excellent evening in front of the television set or not, as the case may be, slowly drinking a "great" bottle. Little pieces of cheese which are not too strong and cream crackers help to bring out the flavour. Apart from wine professionals and the tramps under the Pont-Neuf in Paris, I am not aware that tasting is practised the livelong day. In the beginning of the sixties, Frank Ténot used to compère the radio programme "For jazz-lovers" on Europe No 1. He used to leave the studio about two or three o'clock in the morning, worn out. So he would go back home and relax with a well-chosen cheese and a very good bottle of a great wine which he drank slowly, alone or with two or three friends. That was a good way of appreciating wine.

As regards vintages, I have already made two apparently contradictory statements. The first is that there are no more bad vintages. The second is that Margaux is particularly sensitive to variations in the weather. These two assertions are mutually complementary. This means that today technique in cultivation and vinification can to a large extent correct the deficiencies of the weather. It also means that from one year to another, a greater range of marked differences can be observed in Margaux wines than in the majority of the other appellations. In other words, my dear Marquis, the organ of Margaux is capable of playing with every possible combination of stops, in all the major or minor keys, ranging right from the bassoon to the piccolo and can give us heavenly sounds... its music will always be beautiful.

I am not a stickler for ageing. Although I happily leave all the honours for young wines to Beaujolais (they make me think of those beautiful African girls of twelve years old who, when they reach twenty-four, are already old women), I acknowledge that you can none the less take great delight in drinking a young Margaux wine. Many distinguished Bordeaux people and men from the wine trade on the Quai des Chartrons would not dream of moistening their lips with a great Médoc which is less than ten years old. English

◄ Shad fishing is a traditional activity in the Haut-Médoc. Salmon is also caught, though in small quantities.

amateurs are even more conservative. The success of auction sales of extremely old vintages at Christie's in London is notorious, but we should not confuse museum pieces and the dream fantasies of people who are merely collectors with the works of art which the vignerons-cum-artists put within our reach every year.

The year following bottling is a critical period. It is preferable in nearly all cases to wait at least twelve months before uncorking what has just been corked. Formerly, this waiting period was much longer. Wines suffered from "bottle sickness". In the Gironde, secondary fermentation, known as "malolactic", had for long been badly understood and controlled. People did not know when this sickness would occur. Its symptoms were a disagreeable discharge of carbonic gas, a cloudy appearance, a smell of oxidation and a change in flavour. This used to last for a few months, sometimes for a whole year or even two. Now the "malolactic" follows directly on after the alcoholic fermentation, almost without any break. At the moment of bottling, the wine generally is no longer at risk from reactions of this type. None the less, the trauma of being in a glass prison exists and a rest cure is salutary.

The "off-years" should be drunk rapidly for they will soon lose their substance. But they can be delicious. My grandfather used to say: "I often prefer an off-year from a great *cru* to a great year from a little *cru*." Without taking this idea too literally, you can experience a subtle pleasure in tasting a Margaux wine from an off-year when it is three or four years old. I would say that it is "the rich man's Beaujolais". Amateurs are still keen on having their "vintage chart", with its ratings indicated by stars or by a graduated scale of 1 to 10 or 20. They are useful guides, but they are too generalized. There are individual successes (or failures) which prove the error of systematizing judgements. But seeing that this type of oversimplification is in vogue, I will now draw you an extremely simple diagram, which moreover has been proved true:

$$
\text{Success rating for the vintage}
\begin{cases}
5 & \!\!\!\text{---} 15 \\
4 & \!\!\!\text{---} 9 \\
3 & \!\!\!\text{---} 6 \\
2 & \!\!\!\text{---} 3 \\
1 & \!\!\!\text{---} 3
\end{cases}
\text{Number of years' ageing}
$$

At the bottom of the scale, the time indication is rather an optimum than a minimum. At the top of the scale, it is the other way

round.

In medio stat virtus. A Margaux wine in an off-year is "drinkable" after six years' ageing, but a wine like 1975 can be drunk in thirty years.

Thirty years ago, we were producing the 1953s and 55s which today are superb bottles. Thirty years ago, work on the vines was done with oxen and horses. Thirty years ago, the wines aged in the wood and bottling was done entirely by hand: drawing off, corking, sealing, labelling, wrapping in paper and casing in straw... when the 75s come to peak condition, we shall be in another century. What methods of cultivation and vinification will be being used then? Mechanization has already overtaken the vineyards and the cellars. Certain *crus* in Margaux use the mechanical harvester. We must move with the times. The speed with which the machine can be brought into play at the optimum moment of the grapes' maturity and the economy which mechanization represents are cogent arguments for their use. But the machine does not sort the grapes and it devours leaves. It is no longer the work of man. Diffusing powdered sulphur or other chemical products to protect the vines was done by a machine which could already pulverize. Today this machine can spray... and the pruning machine – yes, there is one – exists in prototype. Its microprocessors are making as much progress as other robots. They are in the process of memorizing the Guyot double system of pruning as practised in the Médoc. As for the tasting machine... with a well-written computer program, it should be capable today of conjugating and declining all the vocabulary of the oenological world. But for the time being, men hold to the expression "sensory assessment" and it is they who have the last word. "So the taster goes from wine to wine, from book to book and from strength to strength. His knowledge widens and deepens. For over twenty years, the developments in the science of tasting have been concentrated on the actual mechanism of the sense of taste, thanks to the work of Le Magnen, and, at the instigation of Vedel, the drawing up of a more complete and precise vocabulary to do with taste. The style of the art of commentary has been perfected with the Chauvets, the Costes, the Goffards and the Puisais" (Emile Peynaud: *Le Goût du vin,* 1980).

Even if progress does not always appear to be moving towards perfection, I am tempted to paraphrase Professor Peynaud saying that "the style of the Margaux vigneron's art has been perfected with the Boyers, the Guillemets, the Lurtons and the Zugers". Margaux

---

In winter, after pruning, the vine twigs are collected, any damaged acacia support-stakes (called "carrassonnes") are replaced and the two remaining branches (called "astes") are trained along the guide-wire consistency.   ▶   81

does not claim to escape the laws of evolution. On the contrary, its claim would rather be to point out a better road towards a better viticultural world. Over the ages, genius makes its mark. There is no reason to suppose that it has finished its course.

*

One of Ausonius's letters to his friend Theon:
"My conscience has been troubling me for not having written to you for some time – a silence you do not deserve, Theon, dear friend and corpulent testimony of a mighty intellect in a mighty mortal frame. The rude winter is over and I wonder what delights spring

can bring if I do not have the support of a cheering companion. And though I admit that the Academy of Bordeaux has granted me the honour of being Professor Intendant of Rhetoric, with Acilius Glabrio as my assistant, and Nepotiamus, Victorius and a phalanx of underlings whose monstrous ignorance matches only their puffed-up pretensions to know everything, yet I am weary now and anxious for your company to inspire me with new enthusiasm for life. It is not too late to go to gather some three hundred or so of those exquisite little oysters from the sea-bed between Dumnitonus and Noviomagus. You know perfectly well that I will eat half of them myself. I will see to everything else. Philo will bring my wine from Lucaniac and I will ask him to put by four ducks for Valentinus while our friend Julius will see to the rest. Come quickly by boat to our rendezvous. The tide gliding its way to Bordeaux will bring you to the hot springs of Marojalum. Here in this blissful spot, far from the crush and din of the city, I will await your arrival in twelve days from now. Farewell. Your friend, Ausonius."

I do not guarantee the authenticity of this document which has remained unpublished to this day. But every detail mentioned agrees with what we know of the great poet. But then, we do not know everything.

The "hot springs of Marojalum", otherwise known as "Marojallia", were the seventh of Ausonius's eight properties listed by Jullian, Piper, Schenkl and Etienne. Up to the present time, no site has been identified with certainty. Many landmarks all seem to support the hypothesis that in the fourth century Margaux was a Gallo-Roman spa. Its location here would seem to be confirmed by the indications given by Ausonius about his comings and goings (mainly by river). The point of confluence of the Garonne and the Dordogne at the Bec d'Ambès was at that time slightly further upstream and Margaux was practically opposite Bourg. The ports of Macau and Margaux were busy and crossings to the town of Bourg (Burgus) took place almost daily. I also tend to believe the theory which sites Ausonius's principal villa on the hills of Bourg. So he could spend some time at "Marojallia" before going back over the estuary to Bourg to see to the running of the largest of his estates.

If toponymy is an exact science, the phonetic change of Marojallia to Margaux is perfectly acceptable. At Margaux, there is a locality called Maragnac. The principal brook of the commune, the Lestonat, was at one time called Magnole. The centre of the village as we know it today between the town hall and Château Malescot was called La Maillolle. This is not far, etymologically speaking, from Ausonius's "Marojallia". Château de La Mothe, which existed before Château Margaux, was constructed very close to the river, perhaps in the thirteenth or fourteenth century. This means that the left bank of the Garonne was about half a mile further south west than it is today. The Marojallia (or Maillolle) must have formed a rather wide canal to take small boats assuring inshore traffic. We know that as from the seventeenth century increased silting up on this side of the river obliged the public authorities to look for other ports to serve Margaux. Moreover, at Margaux there is an outcrop

Throughout the pruning period, work on the vineyards is punctuated by smoke signals coming from the bonfires at the end of the rows. But all the vignerons keep back a few bundles... for cooking their steaks.

▲ Traditionally, bundles of willow twigs, called "vimes", are used to train the vines, but they are disappearing, giving way to synthetic materials. On the loamy soils and along the streams, young willows are grown to produce these "vimes".

◄ Pruning vines is a real art. Here at Château du Tertre at Arsac, we see how the vigneron goes about it. After pruning, he will train the vines himself so that they shall be exactly as he wants them.

of chalky rock, unique in this part of the Médoc. It is a thick layer of lacustrine limestone known as Plassac limestone. This little geological phenomenon was responsible for the spring called the Fontenelle, whose waters have gushed forth every day since the time of Ausonius and which gives the purest water in the area. Above the spring, a tiny square of woodland has grown, standing all by itself in the middle of a vineyard, probably on the ruins of a very old construction (there are many half-buried stones to be seen, overgrown with moss, but this place was used as a tip for a long time).

In short, I have every reason to believe that the "hot springs of Marojalum", where Ausonius used to carouse with his friends, were not far from Block 165, Section A on Margaux's Land Register, if anyone wishes to take the trouble to dig into the question.

*

History can be manipulated in a thousand-and-one ways and nobody is better at sleight of hand than the people of Margaux. Over the last centuries they have made *crus* appear and disappear again with a skill reminiscent of Robert Houdini and his magic wand. For

---

▲ *All viticultural methods have developed with new techniques. Only the vigneron's hand movements as he meticulously prunes his vines have not changed over the centuries.*

a decade or two, the marquis would give way to the viscount. The latter would create a majestic vineyard and build a mansion fit for an archduke. After this, the estate would decline again. Many of the *grands crus* in the Médoc have seen the cards cut and shuffled more or less in secret many times, and many times, more or less openly, they have made their discards. If the cards had to be redistributed to reform the "hands" of 1855, the date of the famous classification, the viticultural Land Register would risk implosion.

But the numerous exchanges, mutations and acquisitions should be considered as continuing improvements over the generations. Within the area today delimited by the Margaux AOC, many parcels of land have changed their labels as a result of being absorbed by the *crus classés* or the leading *crus bourgeois*. The extension of large estates is basically an excellent thing for, with a few rare exceptions, it has the effect of improving the average level of quality. History has shown us this with the work of the likes of Aulède, Rausan, Lascombes, Brane, Kirwan, etc., and we see it continued by the proprietors of today.

Great wine is an individual work of art. In the school of Margaux, it has reached perfection.

Defining the style of Margaux wines

At Château Lascombes on April 15, 1988, an exceptional gathering of fifty of some of the world's best wine-tasters took place. The majority of proprietors and growers in the Margaux appellation had agreed to play the game by providing samples of their production for a blind tasting. But this was not a competition aimed at classifying the wines in an order of merit. The idea was to describe the wines tasted in an academic way without awarding them points. To do this, each taster was given a sheet listing a vocabulary of 150 permitted words. During the course of the morning, ten *crus* of the same vintage were brought to every table, at which there were ten tasters. When a *cru* had been tasted, the appraisal sheets were fed into a computer, so enabling the data collected to draw up a synthesis of the individual descriptions, reproduced in the form of a graph. At the end of the tasting session, each table was called on to cite the two wines most typical of the Margaux style, that is ten *crus* all told. These results were then put together in the computer in order to find which words were most often used and to obtain an objective synthesis of the "Margaux style".

*

On the opposite page is a copy of the appraisal sheet. Each taster had to choose three words to describe the appearance of the wine, nine for its olfactory effect, two for the general impression, ten for the taste and one for the persistence of the taste. He had the choice of grading the relative importance of each word chosen on a scale from 1 to 5, according to the number of crosses he marked in the boxes opposite the word. He could also complete his personal description of the wine with his own commentary written in the bottom right-hand corner.

Out of the fifty or so *crus* tasted, the ten wines chosen by the five tables were: for the 1978 vintage, Châteaux Margaux and Palmer;

Defining the style of Margaux wines

A. The Eye [3]

• *Appearance*
A 1 Clear
A 2 Bright
A 3 Thick

• *Hue*
A 4 Pale
A 5 Brick
A 6 Ruby
A 7 Bluish
A 8 Garnet
A 9 Dark

B. The Nose [9]

• *Plant analogies*
B 1 New wood
B 2 Hay
B 3 Grass
B 4 Ivy
B 5 Undergrowth
B 6 Mushroom
B 7 Truffle
B 8 Lime/linden
B 9 Verbena
B 10 Sandalwood
B 11 Resin
B 12 Balsam
B 13 Tea

• *Flower analogies*
B 14 Rose
B 15 Violet
B 16 Iris
B 17 Geranium
B 18 Hawthorn
B 19 Mignonette

• *Fruit analogies*
B 20 Red fruits
B 21 Cherry
B 22 Raspberry
B 23 Redcurrant
B 24 Black fruits
B 25 Blackcurrant
B 26 Blackberry
B 27 Preserved fruit
B 28 Raisin
B 29 Fig
B 30 Peach
B 31 Quince
B 32 Plum
B 33 Date
B 34 Prune
B 35 Banana
B 36 Fresh almonds
B 37 Roasted almonds

• *Spices and aromas*
B 38 Orange peel
B 39 Cinnamon
B 40 Cocoa
B 41 Vanilla
B 42 Coffee
B 43 Caramel
B 44 Tobacco

• *Animal analogies*
B 45 Musky
B 46 Venison
B 47 Game
B 48 Offal
B 49 Leather
B 50 Milk

• *Mineral and miscellaneous analogies*
B 51 Amber
B 52 Tar
B 53 Metallic
B 54 Ink
B 55 Rancio

C. Overall Impression [2]

C 1 Closed
C 2 Reticent
C 3 Open
C 4 Developed
C 5 Fully developed
C 6 Violent
C 7 Spare
C 8 Fresh
C 9 Young
C 10 Biting
C 11 Vigorous
C 12 Baked
C 13 Concentrated
C 14 Old
C 15 Tired

D. The Palate [10]

• *Intensity*
D 1 Limited
D 2 Slight
D 3 Reserved
D 4 Discreet
D 5 Lively
D 6 Sinewy
D 7 Filled out
D 8 Ardent
D 9 Rough
D 10 Generous
D 11 Alcoholic
D 12 Powerful
D 13 Full
D 14 Rich
D 15 Solid

• *Structure*
D 16 Tannic
D 17 Full-bodied
D 18 Good backbone
D 19 Full
D 20 Complex
D 21 Well-balanced
D 22 Harmonious
D 23 Melting
D 24 Fleshy
D 25 Soft
D 26 Hollow
D 27 Tight
D 28 Closed
D 29 Hard
D 30 Astringent

• *Pleasure*
D 31 Ripe
D 32 Smooth
D 33 Stout
D 34 Round
D 35 Unctuous
D 36 Heavy
D 37 Mild
D 38 Straightforward
D 39 Clean
D 40 Acid
D 41 Thick
D 42 Common

• *Masculine connotations*
D 43 Charming
D 44 Sincere
D 45 Virile
D 46 Distinguished
D 47 Full of character
D 48 Seductive
D 49 Well-bred
D 50 Distinctive
D 51 Frank
D 52 Sturdy
D 53 Rustic
D 54 Flattering

• *Feminine connotations*
D 55 Caressing
D 56 Supple
D 57 Delicate
D 58 Tender
D 59 Silky
D 60 Velvety
D 61 Satiny
D 62 Lacy
D 63 Elegant
D 64 Classy
D 65 Graceful
D 66 Exquisite

E. Persistence [1]
E 1 Short
E 2 Brief
E 3 Long
E 4 Persistent
E 5 Lingering

Comments:

Table no.
Wine no.
Taster

© Jacques Legrand SA

for the 1981 vintage, Angludet and Issan; for the 1982 vintage, Malescot Saint-Exupéry and La Gurgue; for the 1985 vintage, which was divided out among two tables, Brane-Cantenac, Cantenac Brown, Lascombes and Rausan-Ségla.

This experiment was considered very interesting and the general conclusion to be drawn was that Margaux wines are not as "femi-

The 50 tasters in front of Château Lascombes with the late Alain Maurel and Roger Zuger.
First row, seated, from left to right: Jean-Luc Pouteau, Roger Zuger, David Molyneux-Berry, Michael Broadbent, Bernard Ginestet (mayor of Margaux), Fumiko Arisaka, Alain Maurel (president of "Alexis Lichine & Co."), Jacques Puisais, Maryse Allarousse and Daniel Lawton.
Second row: Serge Tonneau, Robert Goffard, Joseph Bessemans, Edmund Penning-Rowsell, Hubrecht Duijker, Chantal Lecouty, Michel Dovaz, Jon Winroth, Steven

Spurrier, Jancis Robinson, René Vanetelle (Lascombes), Philippe Borguignon, Jean Lenoir, Harald Ecker, David Peppercorn, Anthony Rose and Joanna Simon.
Third row: Hubert Monteilhet, Georges Lepré, Raymond Dumay, Robert Joseph, Jacques Luxey, Pascal Ribereau-Gayon, Jean-Noël Boidron and Marc Quertinier.
Fourth row: Peter Thustrup, Anders Rottorp, Martin Kilchmann, Andreas Keller, Raoul Salama, Jo Gryn, Jacques Boissenot, Michel Bettane, Colin Parnell, Pierre Casamayor, Alain Mozès, Louis Binnemans, Hélène Durand, Patrick Fievez, Patrice Pottier and Michel Vidoudez.

93

nine" as has been claimed up to now. There goes another misconception! What is more, this was undoubtedly the first time a group of experienced tasters were able to work together with a view to describing the style of the wines of an *appellation d'origine contrôlée*. This example should be followed in other wine-producing regions. To finish, we should thank the sporting gesture of Château Lascombes for having agreed to play the game and for being our host.

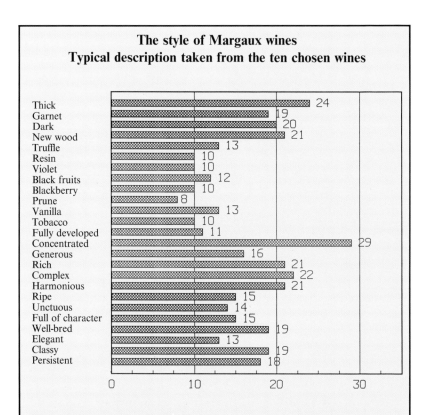

The style of Margaux wines
Typical description taken from the ten chosen wines

Description	Value
Thick	24
Garnet	19
Dark	20
New wood	21
Truffle	13
Resin	10
Violet	10
Black fruits	12
Blackberry	10
Prune	8
Vanilla	13
Tobacco	10
Fully developed	11
Concentrated	29
Generous	16
Rich	21
Complex	22
Harmonious	21
Ripe	15
Unctuous	14
Full of character	15
Well-bred	19
Elegant	13
Classy	19
Persistent	18

Margaux wines are distinguished by an elegant **intense and deep garnet** colour. Their bouquet often has perfumes of **new wood** and aromas in which **truffle, black fruits** (particularly **blackberry**) predominate, with hints of **vanilla** and **tobacco**. There is also the scent of **resin** together with **violets and plum**. Margaux wines are particularly concentrated and appear **rich** and **generous**. They have a **complex** but **harmonious** structure and are generally very **ripe** and **unctuous**. Margaux wines are notable for their **breeding**, their positive **character** and their **development**. They are wines of great **distinction** and have considerable **elegance**. The **persistence** of their flavour is quite remarkable.

Catalogue
of crus

The term *cru classé* is used only in describing the *crus* belonging to the official 1855 classification. The date is not repeated each time the classification is mentioned.

 The number of coloured glasses beside a *cru* gives an idea of the value for money it represents. This estimation, while arrived at as objectively as possible, is naturally subject to discussion and to charge.

 This symbol denotes an exceptional wine.

Certain châteaux have one or more different labels for other wines produced by the property (for example wines from young vines). Such wines are followed by an arrow which indicates the château of origin.

This symbol indicates that a particular name is the secondary wine of a larger estate.

CB This denotes château-bottled.

Angludet (Château d')

cru exceptionnel

Communes: Cantenac and Arsac. **Proprietor:** SC Château d'Angludet. Director: Peter A. Sichel, assisted by Didier Chauvet. **Size of vineyard:** 32 hectares. **Average age of vines:** 16 years. **Varieties:** 50% cabernet-sauvignon, 35% merlot, 8% cabernet-franc, 7% petit-verdot. **Production:** 150,000 bottles CB. **Direct sales and by mail order:** in France. Monsieur & Madame Peter A. Sichel, 33460 Margaux. Tel. 56 88 71 41. **Marketing:** through the trade; Maison Sichel, 19 quai de Bacalan, 33000 Bordeaux.

Of all the noble houses in the Margaux appellation, that of Angludet is undoubtedly one of the oldest. Today attached administratively to Cantenac, the estate of Angludet used to have a part of its land in Arsac, and its total area was greatly superior to the 80 hectares of today. The knights of Angludet were proud and irascible in the purest mediaeval tradition. As far back as the twelfth century, Bertrand d'Angludet was said to have the most distinguished lineage in the Médoc. In 1313, an Angludet categorically refused to swear faith to the powerful Baron of Blanquefort. Edward II of England accepted him round his round table, the more readily because of his vassal's excellent wine. In the fifteenth century, a squire named Makanen won an Angludet heiress. A good catch.

Up to the French Revolution, this château was a *cru classé*: its wines were as expensive as those of today's third and fourth *crus* of the Médoc. The proprietor was a certain citizen Legras. In his political zeal, he had rechristened his *cru* "La République"! His four children were, logically enough, placed under the protection of the good fairy Marianne.* Then in 1791 after the death of their father, they democratically divided the estate out among themselves in four parts, thus swallowing up the *cru*'s fame of which each member devoured a quarter. This is how the Legras family displayed their patriotism and as a result, Angludet failed to be classified in 1855. For a period of a hundred years, it could well have been called The Hydra, but in 1892 Jules Jadouin reintegrated the estate once more. His son-in-law, Jacques Lebègue, set about restoring the family fortunes and in the twenties, Angludet resurfaced. But not for long, for the thirties and forties were far from being a success, and the then proprietor, Monsieur Six, an industrialist from the north of France, was more interested in the butter and eggs his farmer used to send him every week. There were more complications in the fifties, when Madame Rolland, who was also the proprietor of Château Coutet in Barsac, saw her new vineyard destroyed by frost. In 1960, Lucien Lurton bought half the vines, the other half falling into English hands through the firm of Sichel.

Peter and Diana Sichel live at Angludet. Thanks to them it is a real little "piece of England". One of the brooks has been widened. The swans float proudly on it and little ducks swim happily about. The turf, sloping gently down, is as fine as that at Wimbledon. At weekends, they play cricket. A few Welsh ponies roaming free complete the picture of life in the country. If you are taken round the cellars, you should reply in English, *"Thank you"*. The vineyard, surrounded by Giscours, Brane-Cantenac and Kirwan, is a splendid plateau of heavy gravelly soil in which even couch grass refuses to grow, leaving the vines to reign supreme. Six *crus* in the Médoc, unjustifiably overlooked in the 1855 classification, were awarded

* Name given to the Republic after a secret Republican society sworn to overthrow the Second Empire. (Translator's footnote)

At Angludet, the vines are part of a landscape which exudes British romanticism.

one (devalued) franc damages in 1932 by the Bordeaux brokers: the (officious) permission to claim the title of *"cru exceptionnel"*. The wine of Angludet surprises by its vigour, rather unusual in the Margaux appellation. It has a deep colour and is rather compact and tannic. It is good value. Just like the British gentry, it is naturally "conservative", which means that it develops slowly but surely and that age gradually gives it the discreet charm of the nobility. Moreover, that is why it is best to approach the château directly if you want to buy some.

Baudry (Château) ♟ → *Desmirail*

Bel Air-Marquis d'Aligre (Château)

cru exceptionnel

Communes: Soussans and Margaux. **Proprietor:** Pierre Boyer. 33460 Margaux. Tel. 56 88 70 70. **Size of vineyard:** 17 hectares. **Average age of vines:** 35 years. **Varieties:** 30% cabernet-sauvignon, 35% merlot, 20% cabernet-franc, 15% petit-verdot. **Production:** "a small amount", declares Monsieur Boyer modestly. **Marketing:** through the trade and direct sales.

In the nineteenth century, these stamped bottles were exclusive.

Here too is another château overlooked by the 1855 classification. You would think that the members of the panel of Napoleon III's Universal Exhibition were afraid of handing out too many laurels to the wines of Margaux. Bel Air-Marquis d'Aligre is a *cru exceptionnel*. Its right to be called "Margaux" was legally recognized on March 3, 1898. The working buildings are in Soussans and the distinguished vineyard lies between Margaux and Soussans.

Pierre Boyer is a purist. He never seeks the easy way out. He prefers to produce a small quantity of wine but the best. He often succeeds. The vines are maintained at an average age of 35 years which automatically guarantees quality. He carries on the work of his predecessors who sacrificed yield to high quality. During the whole of the nineteenth century, not a drop of Bel Air-Marquis d'Aligre was sold to the wine trade. The Marchioness of Pomereu and the Marquis of Aligre produced their nectar to be served at their own table and to offer a few bottles to their many friends. A handful of Parisian restaurateurs were allowed to be entered on this list. These very remarkable bottles could be identified by a stamp moulded into the glass on the shoulder of each bottle in the old-fashioned style (only the *grands crus* could afford such luxury at that time). In the same way, a "reverse side" label was moulded onto the back with this inscription: *Défendu d'en laisser* (it is forbidden to leave any). The initiates of the time called the wine of Château Bel Air-Marquis d'Aligre "the forbidden Margaux". But before leaving any, it was practically impossible to buy any.

Today, Pierre Boyer allows you to taste it but there is not enough for everybody. You can believe me if I say that he truly regrets this. The wine is sappy, lively, rather intense and generally very fruity. Sometimes it has surprising hints of liquorice. It is a worthwhile bottle to have in a good cellar.

Bellegarde (Château) ⚱ → *Siran*

Bellevue de Tayac (Château) ⚑→ Haut-Tayac

Bigos (Clos de)

Commune: Soussans. **Proprietor:** André Mestrie. **Size of vineyard:** 80 ares. **Average age of vines:** 25 to 30 years. **Varieties:** 40% cabernet-sauvignon, 60% merlot. **Direct sales:** tel. 56 88 35 45, **and by mail order:** in France and abroad. André Mestrie, Bourriche, Soussans, 33460 Margaux. *One of the smallest crus of the appellation, ideal for the collector of rarities.*

Bory (Château) ⚑

→ Angludet

Boyd-Cantenac (Château)

3e cru classé

Commune: Cantenac. **Proprietor:** GFA of Château Boyd-Cantenac and Pouget. Tenant and estate manager: Pierre Guillemet, who is responsible for the management and vinification under the direction of Professor Emile Peynaud. **Size of vineyard:** 18 hectares. **Average age of vines:** 30 years. **Varieties:** 67% cabernet-sauvignon, 7% cabernet-franc, 20% merlot, 6% verdot. **Production:** 85,000 bottles CB. **Direct sales and by mail order:** in France. Château Boyd-Cantenac, Cantenac, 33460 Margaux. Tel. 56 88 30 58. **Marketing:** through the Bordeaux trade: Dubos Frères, André Quancard, Moueix-Export, Descaves, Sté des Vins de France, Ginestet, Merlaut, Beyerman, Gautreau, Barrière.

For the layman, it is sometimes difficult to choose the wine he wants on a wine list and be sure of getting it right. Even restaurateurs can mistake one label for another. In Cantenac, three *crus classés* all have similar sounding names and can easily trick the ears of unsuspecting foreigners. They are Boyd-Cantenac, Brane-Cantenac and Cantenac Brown. In 1754, Master Jacques Boyd, the king's equerry, who lived on the Quai des Chartrons in Bordeaux, bought several plots of land in the parish of Cantenac. And so the estate of the Boyd family was born, a family which became linked by marriage with the Browns. (John Lewis has left to posterity many portraits – the likenesses are striking – of dogs, cats and horses, highly sought after by collectors). In 1806, a family crisis of the type, "All is over, my son-in-law", brought about the Browns achieving total control. The affair was complicated. The judges of the 1855 classification viewed the case globally, putting the wine bearing the name "Boyd" in the third group, with the mention: "other proprietors". Five years later, things became clearer, to the advantage of Brown-Cantenac, and Boyd was to fall into oblivion for some fifty years. It was Fernand Ginestet who, after Abel Laurent, put the *cru*'s land back to what it had been and restored it to its former distinction. His son, Pierre Ginestet, acting discreetly in the background, helped to bring this success about. Just as at Pauillac the vineyard of the Baron de Pichon de Longueville (2nd *cru classé*) was divided into two distinct *crus* (Baron and Comtesse de Lalande), the original estate of the equerry Jacques Boyd created two 3rd *crus*. Today, Boyd-Cantenac belongs to the Guillemet family.

Pierre Guillemet is an enlightened grower who knows his land and his vines inside out. The dominance of the cabernet-sauvignon and his preference for a feeble yield (an average of barely 35 hectolitres per hectare) result in a very high class wine which is sappy, full of finesse and charm. It should be said that Professor Emile Peynaud comes along to put his little pinch of knowledge into the vats during vinification. Boyd-Cantenac could well be reproached for the austerity of its label. In fact, tribute should be paid to this modesty which is extremely rare nowadays for when all is said and done, it is not the casket which makes the jewel.

Like a private garden, the vineyard of Brane stretches to the very walls of the château.

Brane-Cantenac (Château)

Commune: Cantenac. **Proprietor:** Lucien Lurton. Vine-yard manager: Serge Branas. Cellar master: Yves Blanchard. **Size of vineyard:** 85 hectares. **Average age of vines:** 25 years. **Varieties:** 70% cabernet-sauvignon, 15% cabernet-franc, 13% merlot, 2% petit-verdot. **Production:** 300,000 bottles CB. **Direct sales and by mail order:** in France. Château Brane-Cantenac, Cantenac, 33460 Margaux. Tel. 56 88 70 20. **Marketing:** through all the large firms in Bordeaux.

People always speak of the Baron de Brane as of one single, suddenly created personage, a rather legendary figure who was born one fine day and called Brane. In 1693, Bertrand de Brane was King's Counsellor and Lord High Chancellor of the Court of Aydes in Guienne. His son, Joseph, was the distinguished proprietor of the *cru* Mouton in the commune of Pauillac. A century before being Mouton-Rothschild, this *cru* was called Brane-Mouton. At that time, Château Brane-Cantenac was called quite simply Gorce (or Gorse). It was Bertrand's grandson, Hector, who earned the nickname of "Napoleon of the Vines". He reigned

over an empire and was the first to organize viticulture in the way we understand it today. It seems that it was he who was at the origin of the present day cabernet-sauvignon. After selling Mouton, he bought the *cru* of Gorce from citizen Guy and invested considerable sums of money. In 1838 he wrote: "I thought I ought to give my name to a creation which is wholly mine. If the name of Gorce is rightly appreciated in Bordeaux and elsewhere, that of Brane is not less so... I am hoping gradually to let the name of Gorce fall into oblivion and to take it under the wing of Brane-Cantenac." Brane-Cantenac rose to fame with dazzling speed. Within thirty years, it became a sort of curiosity in the viticultural world because of its modern approach in the search for perfection. But it seems that the efforts of Baron Hector were not financially viable. His son, Jacques Maxime, sold the estate again in 1866 under conditions highly disadvantageous to himself.

CHATEAU
BRANE CANTENAC
1ᵉʳ VIN

1975

The gravel slopes of Château Brane-Cantenac are among the highest in all the appellation. They have a fairly uniform depth of thirty to thirty-six feet. This estate is remarkably unified. At the beginning of this century, it belonged to the Société des Grands Crus de France, which owned ten or so estates such as Coutet, Issan, Lagrange... The Récapet-Lurton family, shareholders in Château Margaux in 1922 after the departure of the Duke de La Trémoïlle, became absolute owners of Brane-Cantenac in 1926, at which date the Société des Grands Crus divided up its assets and sold them at auction. Today it is Lucien Lurton, François's son, who is the owner of this great 2nd *cru classé*, the only one in the commune of Cantenac and one of the five in the Margaux appellation. Succeeding "Napoleon", Lucien Lurton is a modern "Marquis of Carabas" of the vines. To mention only the Margaux appellation, he reigns over some 430 hectares (the whole of the commune of Margaux has 630 hectares), of which approximately 145 are under vines and produce the following wines: Château Brane-Cantenac, Château Durfort-Vivens, Château Desmirail. Château La Tour de Bessan, Château Notton-Baury, and the *Domaines* de Cure-Bourse and de Fontarney are subsidiary names for smaller wines.

But if he felt like taking you on a guided tour of all the proprietor's estates, the Puss-in-Boots on duty would also have to take you to the following châteaux: Château Villegeorge in Avensan, Château Bouscaut in Cadaujac, Château Haut-Nouchet in Martillac, Château Climens in Barsac, Château Doisy-Dubroca in Barsac, Château Camarsac in Camarsac... and other places, uncovered at low tide where the malbec grapes are harvested with waders.

Whatever the case, Lucien Lurton is a pioneer of modern viticulture. He arbitrates over what is intensive and extensive. He lives intensively, forever developing extensively. He is not a man to take things easy. He is a tireless conqueror and, while contemplating all the jewels in his crown, could it be that he still has a certain nostalgia for Château Margaux, the only one perhaps, in his opinion, worthy of him? Following Stendhal, men have been able to unleash their passions and diversify them. None the less, to own three *crus classés* in Margaux is not something to be found every day of the week. There is work enough to fill his life and two thousand tonneaux. The wine of Brane-Cantenac is smooth, silky and feminine to the last drop. It is a filigree of tenderness. Rather capricious by nature, it can deceive but the next time round it will display a genial charm.

Cantenac Brown (Château)

3e cru classé

Commune: Cantenac. **Proprietor:** SC of Château Cantenac Brown. Estate manager: Aymar du Vivier. Cellar master: André Féménia. Vineyard manager: Raymond Martin. **Size of vineyard:** 42 hectares. **Average age of vines:** 20 years. **Varieties:** 69% cabernet-sauvignon, 6% cabernet-franc, 25% merlot. **Production:** between 200,000 and 225,000 bottles CB. **Direct sales and by mail order:** Château Cantenac Brown, Cantenac, 33460 Margaux. Tel. 56 88 30 07. **Marketing:** all the production is sold directly at the château.

"This château – how fair! – by its lake azure blue/Is Brown-Cantenac, now classed as third *cru.*/Its vines seen afar on the top of the hill/From tempests, alas! have suffered great ill./Fond plaything of men so greedy for gain,/Whose bailiffs severe tried oft to distrain./Yet nought has destroyed its vineyard serene,/And today more than ever, it flourishes green."

Biarnez, that tireless writer of verses on the *grands crus* of the Médoc, has left us these majestic lines written just before the war of 1870, rich in rhyme and resonance. They reflect perfectly the joys and woes of many Bordeaux châteaux which, with the passing generations, economic crises and damaging inheritances, have sometimes known glory and sometimes shame.

The château as such had previously been divorced from all wine-making activity. But now it has once again become wedded to vinification and the working buildings are being improved. The architecture is picturesque. It was constructed as a "folly", that veritable metempsychosis of the English Renaissance, by the animal painter John Lewis Brown who came from an English family of wine merchants. Henri de Toulouse-Lautrec used to spend a lot of time with John Lewis Brown for they both loved good wine, women and their master Princeteau. But however talented he may have been, John Lewis Brown did not make ends meet and he was obliged to sacrifice his wine for his bread. In 1843, in desperate straits, he sold his estate,

Château Cantenac Brown is an architectural curiosity of the region.

The new vat-house at Cantenac Brown is one of the best equipped in the Médoc.

formerly called "Boyd" (see Boyd-Cantenac), in two lots. The Lalandes were at that time notable Chartrons merchants in all their splendour. They bought "Brown" for a song, and set up there with their huge staff, leading a dazzling social life. From vines to vat-house, from vat-house to tonneau and from tonneau to the Danaids,* the likeable heir of this saga, Jean Lawton (the best snipe-shooter on the north side of Bordeaux) resigned himself to selling the vineyard to the du Vivier family. After making a good start to restoring the vineyard, they accepted the important offer made by the Compagnie du Midi, disappointed at having been "pipped at the post" by its great rival Axa for the purchase of Pichon Baron at Pauillac. The firm of Château Cantenac Brown, whose president is Jean-Paul Arnal, was anxious that Aymar du Vivier should still hold the reins of the *cru*. Furthermore, Jean Calvet, the former president of the firm, agreed to occupy his retirement by looking after advertising and marketing. Very substantial investments have been made. In particular, today we can admire the Médoc's most "technological" vat-house. The vineyard manager, my friend Raymond Martin, a former cross-country champion, is part of the team. And quality is in the fore. We can even say that it is gaining a lead over many of Margaux's *crus classés*.

The Danaids of Greek mythology were condemned to the endless task of carrying water in tonneaux perforated like sieves.

Canuet (Château)

cru bourgeois

Up to 1986, Château Canuet's management and vinification were in the hands of Jean and Sabine Rooryck. Since then, this estate of some 10 hectares has been bought by the firm of Château Cantenac-Brown so becoming its second label. The fate of the charming house in the centre of Margaux village is still unknown.

Carabins (Château des)

→ *Ligondras*

Carreyre (Château) ⚲→ *Haut-Tayac*

Castelbruck (Cru de)

Commune: Arsac. **Proprietor:** Marc Raymond. **Size of vineyard:** 3.33 hectares. **Average age of vines:** 6 to 15 years. **Varieties:** traditional. **Production:** 50 hectolitres per hectare. **Direct sales and by mail order:** in France. Cru de Castelbruck, Le Tayet, Macau, 33460 Margaux. Tel. 56 30 42 73. **Marketing:** 3/4 of the production is sold in bulk to the Bordeaux trade.

Marc Raymond is the third generation of a family of growers. The family's vines are in Macau where their Château des Charmilles produces an agreeable "Bordeaux Supérieur" on rich loamy soil. Things might have remained like that for generations to come and Marc Raymond would not have featured in this catalogue. But in his opinion, it was a crying shame to live so close to the Margaux AOC and to have no benefit from it other than drinking a bottle from time to time with friends. It was a crying shame to love being a professional vigneron and wine producer and yet not have the best land possible. It was a crying shame not to be able to demonstrate his skill in planting, ploughing, pruning, sulphating and harvesting the cabernet-sauvignon except in "heavy soils". The weeping is over and the "shame has been turned into glory". Over the last fifteen years, Marc Raymond has created a little vineyard in the Margaux AOC, split up into eight parcels in the commune of Arsac, of which two are at the side of *grands crus classés*. And right was on Marc Raymond's side. His young vines are now giving better and better results.

Charmant (Château)

Communes: Margaux and Soussans. **Proprietor:** René Renon. **Size of vineyard:** 5 hectares. **Average age of vines:** 50% of the vineyard is over 100 years old. **Varieties:** 45% merlots, 50% cabernets, 5% petit-verdot. **Production:** 20,000 bottles CB. **Direct sales and by mail order:** in France and abroad. Château Charmant, 33460 Margaux. **Marketing:** through the trade; Maison Joanne in Carignan, 33370 Tresses.

Since the beginning of the nineteenth century, this little vineyard has been situated between Margaux and Soussans. In 1866, Charles Cocks mentions *"cru Charmant"* belonging to B. Constantin and he lists it among the *"crus artisans"* and "*crus paysans supérieurs*". At that time it was also called Constant-Charmant. The proprietor of today is René Renon, a man of a species which is becoming rare in Margaux. He himself is an "artisan supérieur" living with his vines, for his vines and by his vines. He can speak the regional dialect, knows all the local stories and anecdotes which he can relate with all the talent of a born raconteur, when he feels so inclined. He does not need satellites to know what the weather is going to do tomorrow. Along with his wife Jeanette, he runs his two *crus artisans* – Château Charmant and Château La Galiane (see this name) in Soussans – surrounded by *grands crus*. You might find that the term "château" is less charming than the former designation as *cru*. You might also consider that the label has a family resemblance with that of Château Margaux, but you would be wrong to consider taking the proprietor to litigation, for this is how he modestly announces his proximity to prestigious neighbours. Half of the vineyard is more than one hundred years old. Although it is difficult to be categorical, I think that they are the oldest vines in Margaux. The most remakable thing is that they are direct sets (that is to say, not grafted) of cabernets and merlots with a few carmenères. They give very little wine, but the best. It was René's father, Adonis, who taught him how to prune. The wine finds a happy balance between being sturdily structured yet supple. Sometimes it develops superbly well when it ages and can "match" the greatest *crus* of the area.

Clairefont (Château)

→ *Prieuré-Lichine*

Clos de La Gravière (Château)

Commune: Arsac. **Proprietor:** Monsieur & Madame Mondon. **Size of vineyard:** 2.7 hectares. **Average age of vines:** 25 years. **Varieties:** 1/3 cabernet-franc, 1/3 cabernet-sauvignon, 1/3 merlot. **Production:** 1,000 bottles bottled on the estate, the rest is sold in bulk to the trade. **Direct sales and by mail order:** Monsieur and Madame Mondon, Les Châlets, Avensan, 33480 Castelnau-de-Médoc. Tel. 56 58 20 67. **Marketing:** through the trade.

Avensan is a commune bordering Soussans and Arsac. Half its land is wooded and half under vines. There are good *crus bourgeois* and *crus artisans* to be found there with the "Haut-Médoc" appellation. Monsieur and Madame Mondon live there and run the family estate. But Madame Mondon originates from Arsac. She came into some land of which about three hectares are planted with cabernet-franc, cabernet-sauvignon and merlot. The average age of the vines is a quarter of a century. Splendid. Their late uncle, called Prévôt (the Prévôt family from Arsac not the one from Margaux) should be pleased to look down from heaven to see that his vines are being well tended and his wine well made. Yes, but nothing is perfect. I particularly regret that the quantity of each harvest bottled on the estate is so slender. Just think of it! 1,000 bottles. You should do something about it. For example, drop a line to Madame Mondon after the harvest to ask her to put you two or three cases by. She could hardly refuse you.

Cure-Bourse (Domaine de) ⚱

→ *Durfort Vivens*

Dauzac (Château)

5e cru classé

Commune: Labarde. **Proprietor:** The MAIF. Director: M. Ribes. Technical Director: Mr Michel Dufaure. **Size of vineyard:** 50 hectares. **Average age of vines:** 18 years. **Varieties:** 65% cabernet, 30% merlot, 5% petit-verdot. **Production:** 250,000 bottles CB. **Direct sales and by mail order:** in France and abroad. Château Dauzac, Labarde, 33460 Margaux. Tel. 56 88 32 10. **Marketing:** through the trade.

"The vineyard of Dauzac acquired its fame as far back as the thirteenth century as a dependency of the Monastery of Sainte-Croix-de-Bordeaux..." What an ignoble way this is of trying to make people believe that this fifth *cru classé* in the commune of Labarde was already famous in the Middle Ages! And yet, this is how it is presented in the majority of works which refer to it and in the copious publicity which its previous proprietor M. Chatellier aimed at lovers of antiquities of the wine world. In the thirteenth century, the poor Benedictine monks of the Monastery of Sainte-Croix sought lands where they could settle. They arrived rather late in the day since the canons of Saint-Seurin, Saint-André and other large Bordeaux parishes had split up the best urban and suburban areas amongst themselves. In true evangelical fashion, Sainte-Croix's land-owning policy spread further into the Médoc and elsewhere. Two rural townships, exempt from taxation and known as "sauvetés" were created, one in Macau and one on the west side of Arsac, serving as a refuge for nomads and fugitives. The one in Macau took in what is today the estate of Dauzac. It consisted of a group of hamlets which had been rapidly constructed to enable wanderers to settle, giving them a plot of land to cultivate

Harvesting at La Maqueline at the turn of the century.

and a purpose in life: that of doing "good works". It was actually about 1220–40 that the first vines appeared in Ludon, Macau and Labarde. But they were planted exclusively in loamy soil. I do not think that this historical background contributes in any way to the long-standing fame of the wine we are speaking of here.

The origin of Dauzac is unsure. Its name is said to derive from the Gallo-Roman word *Davius* or *Davinius*, more frequent in the centre of France. This land probably belonged to the seigniory of Lesparre in the fifteenth century and its name took a Gascon form with "Dauzats". The estate marked time until Jean-Baptiste Lynch, the mayor of Bordeaux right at the beginning of the nineteenth century, came on the scene and Dauzac took on the appearance of a fine sizeable vineyard with a charming mansion at the side. Without any possible doubt, it is thanks to the personality of Lynch that Dauzac is a *cru classé* today, even though the estate was sold several years before the classification to a certain Wiebrock who rapidly sold it to Nathaniel Johnston.

Johnston was an extraordinary innovator. It was he who made the first experiments in anti-mildew spraying with the "bouillie bordelaise" (Bordeaux wash). Dauzac was the experimental laboratory and the success of the mixture is well known (lime and copper sulphate mixed in water. It was initially discovered at Ducru-Beaucaillou, but its centenary was celebrated at Dauzac in 1985). The story does not end there. A great enthusiast for the "champagne method", Nathaniel Johnston, himself bubbling over with ideas, had all the wines he could lay his hands on turned into sparkling ones. Following a practice current on the borders of the department of the Marne, he used to press the wines of Dauzac and La Maqueline (a property on loamy soil straddling Labarde and Macau) and without giving them time to colour, had them carried over the river and transformed into "Sparkling Royal Médoc" in his cellars at Bourg-sur-Gironde. Despite several superb successes with traditional vinification, Château Dauzac did not maintain its splendid new-found fame. Its bright day was transformed into an obscure night whose darkness the Bernat family did not succeed in dispelling. In 1964, the Miailhes bought the estate and the vineyard was partially restored. It was hard work.

Today, the MAIF insurance company owns Dauzac. Since the Chatelliers carried out considerable improvements both on the vineyard and in the working buildings, the *cru* increased considerably in value and they preferred to realize their profit. A capital profit made without "insider information". If Count J.-B. Lynch were to come back, he would be gratified. The vineyard is still rather young, but the experience of Professor Peynaud nurtures this wine and ensures its healthy development. Moreover, and this today is the height of luxury, the land at Dauzac has "rested" for two generations. Very few *crus classés* have had this opportunity of taking a holiday. Dauzac has returned to the top range of Margaux wines.

Desmirail (Château)   ♟♟♟♟♟

3e cru classé

Communes: Cantenac and Arsac. **Proprietor:** Lucien Lurton. Cellar master: Philippe Peschka. **Size of vineyard:** 18 hectares. **Average age of vines:** 25 years. **Varieties:** 69% cabernet-sauvignon, 7% cabernet-franc, 23% merlot, 1% petit-verdot. **Production:** 35,000 to 40,000 bottles CB. **Marketing:** through the Bordeaux trade.

"Desmirail's wines are fine and discreet, / Of elegance rare and texture compact, / Whose deep ruby hue announces a heat / Which thrills and delights with its fiery impact."

This is the moment (or never at all) to quote the poet Biarnez concerning this *cru*, for he was grandfather of Robert von Mendelssohn, the proprietor of Desmirail before the 1914 war, and member of a family of Berlin bankers which also produced the famous musician. But the "Midsummer Night's Dream" was a nightmare for the kindly German banker enamoured of French viticulture. His estate was sequestrated and he never set foot again in his Margaux cellars. In 1923, Monsieur Michel (who is in no way related to the archangel and patron saint of the parish church of Margaux) became its proprietor and held it until the beginning of the Second World War. He then sold it off in small portions, like slices of salami sausage and Desmirail disappeared as a *cru*. Paul Zuger bought the château, built in 1860 in the style of Louis XIII by the estate manager of Château Margaux, and several parcels of vines procuring an artificial survival for the name.

Originally, Desmirail had been taken away from the major holdings of the Rauzans as a dowry for the bride of Monsieur Desmirail. If I am not mistaken, it consisted of 14 hectares on a fine gravel slope in Margaux. Monsieur Desmirail was well satisfied. He passed his name onto the daughter of Rauzan du Ribail and to his own *cru*. Now things have changed considerably. The building of Château Desmirail still exists and Jean-Claude Zuger has renamed it Marquis d'Alesme-Becker (see this name), another *cru classé* in Margaux which had no château of its own. For several years Desmirail served as the second label for Château Palmer. After completing a long and phrenetic jigsaw puzzle, in other words, forty years of serene patience, Lucien Lurton reconstructed the vineyard which today is supposed to consist of the original 18 hectares of vines featured on the 1855 Land Register. In order to give a roof to his "château", he bought the buildings of Port-Aubin in the centre of the village of Cantenac. These had flourished when wines from the alluvial soils were in demand from the trade towards the end of the eighteenth century. We should admire the perseverance of Lucien Lurton and his feel for the land. Without him, Desmirail could well have completely disappeared. Combining oriental philosophy and a Christian conscience, he is a master (vintner) of the Japanese game of "Go". We should also admire Lucien Lurton's keen business sense: his total production of Margaux wines is divided out among three *crus classés* (Château Brane-Cantenac, Château Durfort-Vivens, Château Desmirail) and several subsidiary labels, Domaine de Fontarney being the second label of Desmirail.

Desmirail is dead. Long live Desmirail!

Deyrem-Valentin (Château)

cru bourgeois

Commune: Soussans. **Proprietor:** Jean Sorge. **Size of vineyard:** 11 hectares. **Average age of vines:** 30 years. **Varieties:** 50% merlot, 45% cabernet-sauvignon, 5% malbec, petit-verdot and cabernet-franc. **Production:** 70,000 bottles CB. **Direct sales and by mail order:** in France. Château Deyrem-Valentin, Soussans, 33460 Margaux. Tel. 56 88 35 70. **Marketing:** through the trade. 70% of the production goes for export (U.S.A., Switzerland, G.B., Germany, Denmark, Holland, Belgium).

This is a good *cru bourgeois* whose vineyard is situated at Marsac in the commune of Soussans in the vicinity of Lascombes, Malescot and the two Labégorces. Jean Sorge's home and his cellars are in Soussans. His grandfather, Maurice Blanc, bought this little estate when it was sold at auction by court order in 1928. Deyrem-Valentin is the name of a former proprietor whose lineage has been lost in the mists of time, though it is known that he himself used to represent Soussans on the borough council at Margaux under the First Republic. Jean Sorge runs his estate himself. He is thoroughly conversant with all aspects of the work and nothing daunts him. He runs his 11 hectares of vines prudently, calmly, thoughtfully, without fuss and very efficiently. Although the wine sometimes lacks body, it is remarkable for its bouquet and finesse. It is entirely typical of the wines from Marsac which, as we have noted elsewhere, is the best part of Soussans. The whole of the harvest is château bottled.

Durfort-Vivens (Château)

2e cru classé

Commune: Margaux. **Proprietor:** Lucien Lurton. Cultivation supervisor: Michel Branas. Cellar master: Guy Birot. **Size of vineyard:** 20 hectares. **Average age of vines:** 25 years. **Varieties:** 80% cabernet-sauvignon, 12% cabernet-franc, 8% merlot. **Production:** 90,000 bottles CB. **Direct sales and by mail order:** in France. Château Durfort-Vivens, 33460 Margaux. Tel. 56 88 70 20. **Marketing:** through the trade; Descaves, Nicolas, Agence Igor (in Paris), Moueix, Hédiard, etc.

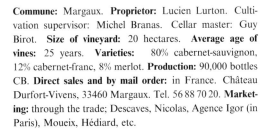

The first traces of the Counts of Durfort de Duras in Margaux are to be found in about the middle of the twelfth century. This powerful family had numerous estates all over the province of Guienne and in particular in what is today the department of Lot-et-Garonne. In about 1450, Thomas de Durfort was the undisputed lord of Margaux. His estates took in Château de La Mothe (today Château Margaux) and the major part of the land making up the commune. The Montalemberts became the owners of Durfort through matrimonial alliances. In the seventeenth century, the proprietors of Durfort and Margaux engaged in a fierce battle concerning weather-cocks, each denying his neighbour the privileged (lordly) right to install one on his roof. At this period Durfort was linked to Lascombes.

In 1768, the Marchioness de Montalembert divided Durfort between her two nephews, Montbrison and Vivens. Viscount Vivens lost no time in buying his cousin out and, much in the style of the period, he created a model vineyard on his estate which became Durfort-Vivens. During his famous visit to the Bordeaux region in 1787, Thomas Jefferson singled out this *cru* and put it at the head of the "second class", a position which was confirmed by the official classification of 1855. Then there was another marriage, that of Viscount Puységur to a niece of the Vivens family. In 1866, the Puységurs sold Durfort to two excellent viticulturalists, Messieurs Richier and de La Marre. They were the first in the Médoc to replace the wooden laths (also called "perches") to support the vines by metal wires and to introduce the practice of "contract vignerons". In 1895, after a short time in the hands of Messieurs Beaucourt and Delmée, the estate became the property of an important Bordeaux wine-merchant, M. G. Delor. He made considerable extensions both to the land and to the buildings which are today as he enlarged them. Abel Delor sold Château Durfort in 1937 to my father Pierre Ginestet who ran the estate in

conjunction with that of Château Margaux, of which he was then shareholder and

On the way into the village of Margaux: the old cooperage of Durfort-Vivens.

managing director, although the buildings retained their own identity and remained quite separate. After the sale, when Abel Delor handed over the keys of Durfort, he insisted, despite my father's protestations, on going round the property with him, going through the inventory with a fine tooth-comb and pointing out all the various nooks and crannies. When they arrived in the little vaulted cellar attached to the château, my father was astounded to find a large number of carefully arranged bottles, forming a collection of the best vintages produced by the *cru* over a century. "But look," said my father, "you have forgotten to empty this cellar!" "My dear friend," replied Delor, "I could not decently see you settle here after me with an empty cellar!" Half a century later, the rare gallantry of this gesture deserves to be acknowledged. In 1961, my father decided to sell the vineyard and the name to Lucien Lurton, but to retain the château – the dwelling – for his own use. The combined estates of Margaux and Durfort had created a certain ambiguity harmful to the latter which was dubbed "second wine of Château Margaux" and not "Second *cru classé* of Margaux". Superficially innocuous, the nuance was poignant and keenly felt. On the other hand, Lucien Lurton had parcels of vines at Brane-Cantenac which belonged to Durfort on the 1855 Land Register. So the vineyard of Château Durfort-Vivens is now in the expert hands of Lucien Lurton. Along with those of Rausan, the wines are some of the most elegant and delicate in all the Margaux AOC, though one would prefer them to be more consistent.

Eyrins (Château des)

Commune: Margaux. **Proprietor:** Eric Grangerou. **Size of vineyard:** 80 ares. **Average age of vines:** 20 years. **Varieties:** 70% cabernet-sauvignon, 20% merlot, 2% cabernet-franc, 2% malbec, 6% petit-verdot. **Production:** 4,500 to 5,000 bottles CB. 17 barriques. **Visits:** tel. 56 88 95 03. **Direct sales and by mail order:** in France and abroad. Eric Grangerou, 27 cours Pey-Berland, 33460 Margaux. **Marketing:** to friends and acquaintances. *Eric Grangerou is the grandson of Marcel and son of John who were successively cellar masters at Château Margaux. He has taken on the little family estate and makes a successful wine, though limited in production.*

Ferrière (Château)

3e cru classé

Commune: Margaux. **Proprietor:** Jean Merlaut. GFA du Château Ferrière. Leased to Sté Alexis Lichine. **Size of vineyard:** 4.12 hectares. **Average age of vines:** 22 years. **Varieties:** 60% cabernet-sauvignon, 30% merlot, 9% cabernet-franc, 1% petit-verdot. **Production:** 15,000 bottles CB. **Marketing:** Sté Alexis Lichine, 109 rue Achard, 33300 Bordeaux. Tel. 56 50 84 85.

After the fall of Robespierre, Jean Ferrière came back to power and was elected mayor of Bordeaux in 1795. He came from a large and very well-known family. Gabriel Ferrière was a proprietor in Margaux. The *cru* was handed down in unbroken succession until 1914 when Henri Ferrière sold it to Armand Feuillerat who owned Marquis de Terme. Feuillerat's daughter, Madame Durand, leased the estate to Alexis Lichine for Château Lascombes in 1960.

Since then, Ferrière is Lascombe's younger brother. Ten to twenty tonneaux are declared every year under the name of Château Ferrière. The château, situated in the heart of the village opposite Margaux's new school complex, is a beautiful fashionable house constructed in the Médoc style of the eighteenth century.

It is pleasing to see that this good old *cru* has found a new personality thanks to Jean Merlaut.

Fontarney (Domaine de) 🍷

→ Desmirail

Gassies du Vieux-Bourg (Château)

Commune: Arsac. **Proprietor:** Louis Gassies. **Size of vineyard:** 1 hectare. **Average age of vines:** 15 years. **Varieties:** 75% merlot and 25% cabernet-sauvignon. **Production:** 1,000 bottles CB. **Direct sales:** tel. 56 58 81 70, **and by mail order:** in France, Château Gassies du Vieux-Bourg, Arsac, 33460 Margaux. **Marketing:** through the trade.

The noble House of Gassies was extremely important in Margaux and the surrounding areas, especially during the sixteenth and seventeenth centuries. It has left its mark with Château Rauzan-Gassies, a 2nd *cru classé*. But the Château Gassies du Vieux-Bourg has no connection whatsoever with the former lands of the Gassies. This modest vineyard has come down from mother to daughter over the last five generations.

After the war, one of the Montminoux daughters (a very old Arsac family) married Louis Gassies from Pauillac and they decided to tend this parcel of vines themselves, and to give it his personal stamp, he called it after his own name, in the style of Baron de Brane or the Chevalier de Lascombes. Would he have done this had he been called Dupont or Smith? We shall never know.

Louis Gassies still sells his wine in casks, keeping back a small quantity for bottling on site. The Crédit Agricole ought to help finance the vintners of Margaux, great and small alike, to enable them to see the ageing cycle right through and to practise château bottling. This would be to the benefit of both the image of the Margaux AOC and the consumer.

Giscours (Château)

3e cru classé

Commune: Labarde. **Proprietor:** GFA du Château Giscours. **Manager:** Nicolas Tari for SA du Château Giscours. **Estate manager and consultant oenologist:** Lucien Guillemet. **Cultivation supervisor:** J.-P. Laduche. **Cellar master:** G. Sérani. **Size of vineyard:** 80 hectares. **Average age of vines:** 30 years. **Varieties:** 75% cabernet-sauvignon, 20% merlot, 5% cabernet-franc and petit-verdot. **Production:** 350,000 bottles CB. **Direct sales and by mail order:** in France. Château Giscours, Labarde, 33460 Margaux. Tel. 56 88 34 02. **Marketing:** wines distributed through International Distillers and Vintners.

Giscours is the flagship of the commune of Labarde. As you come from Bordeaux, it is in crossing Giscours's superb vineyard that you enter the Margaux

Château Giscours: the impressive château and its working buildings.

appellation. This vineyard, in one almost unbroken stretch, starts at Arsac on the west and extends to Labarde on the east. The château, its imposing out-buildings and magnificent park reign in the middle of a natural hollow. The name Labarde is of Celtic origin meaning "song-bird" or, more precisely, "singing lark". This name turns up again in the little locality "Cantelaude" (*lauda* meaning "lark" in Latin), which is on the south side of the property on the outskirts of the communes of Labarde, Macau and Arsac.

Giscours is probably derived from the Gallo-Roman family name Giscous or Giscos. The Marquis Claude-Anne de Saint-Simon used it as a pseudonym during his exile in Spain in about 1790. Confiscated at the Revolution, Giscours was sold in 1795 to an American, a pioneer of this type of viticultural conquest, whom many were to copy later. Like a great number of its counterparts, Giscours made

its breakthrough in the wine world during the nineteenth century. Marc Promis, Count Pescatore and Edouard Cruse followed one after the other at the head of this exceptional wine-making property. The first renovated the vineyard, the second the château and the third the working buildings. In particular, a distinguished agronomist, M. P. Skavinski, was acting viceroy of Giscours for half a century, bringing his expertise and personal renown to the new-found fame of the *cru*. There then followed half a century in obscurity during which Giscours suffered a decline. The Second World War completely torpedoed the flagship which, disabled, pillaged and abandoned, finally found a man worthy of it in the person of Nicolas Tari. As from 1952, there has been a slow but steady comeback. Originally from Algeria, Nicolas Tari is not afraid of the task he has set himself. The vineyard is being progressively replanted; the cellars, the vat-house, the model farm and château were patched up, then repaired and finally completely restored. The Land Register of the *cru* has been put back to what it was in 1855. Since 1970, Pierre Tari, Nicolas's son, has been helping his father. He has everything needed to ensure the estate's ongoing viability. Since then, a decidedly modern approach has added its voice to the natural harmonies of the *cru* as his father had orchestrated them. Particularly adept at winning over journalists, he also excels in the rôle of *porte-parole*, public relations man, organizer of receptions and banquets, globe-trotting gourmet and polo player. In several years, Giscours has harvested not only good vintages but one of the most voluminous press dossiers of all the *crus classés*. During all this time, a battalion of experts, with Professor Henri Enjalbert at its head, accompanied by Jacques Puisais, Pascal Ribéreau-Gayon and Emile Peynaud, has taken an interest in the Taris' efforts. They observed, considered, gave their report and their advice and the Taris decided to invest in the construction of a 12-hectares lake to complement the natural drainage (already improved during the nineteenth century by the creation of various pools in the park) and to bring a favourable influence to bear on the microclimate. Moreover, its construction made it possible to reform the gravel slopes which had fallen away with erosion. At Giscours, faith moves mountains, creates lakes and... publishes an exclusive newspaper called *Giscours Réalités*, which you would take for an extract from *Vogue* magazine. "A nul autre second" ("second to none") is the Taris' proud motto. Château Giscours, 3rd *cru classé* in 1855, is no longer sure where it should be placed. Has it won its wager to achieve a position beyond compare? That is for consumers to judge. As for myself, I find that the wines of Giscours are well made and highly agreeable. The fact remains that Giscours has become a firm institution. A visit is a must, if only to watch the superb audio-visual presentation now shown to visitors.

Graveline (Château)

Commune: Arsac. **Proprietor:** René Poujeau. **Size of vineyard:** 1 hectare. **Average age of vines:** 20 years. **Marketing:** Messrs. Gardère-Haramboure SA, quai Jean-Fleuret, 33250 Pauillac.

Gravières de Marsac (Château)
→ Marsac Séguineau

Graviers (Château des)

Commune: Arsac. **Proprietor:** SCE des Vignobles Dufourg Landry. **Size of vineyard:** 7 hectares. **Average age of vines:** 20 years. **Varieties:** cabernet-sauvignon and merlot. **Production:** 25,000 bottles CB, the rest sold in bulk. **Direct sales and by mail order:** in France. Château des Graviers, Arsac, 33460 Margaux. Tel. 56 58 89 11. **Marketing:** through the trade in small quantities. *Recent vintages show progress in this newly extended* cru.

Haut Breton Larigaudière (Château)

cru bourgeois supérieur

Commune: Soussans. **Proprietor:** G. de Mour. **Size of vineyard:** 7 hectares (the estate is 9 hectares). **Average age of vines:** 15 years. **Varieties:** 65% cabernet-sauvignon, 35% merlot. **Production:** 40,000 to 50,000 bottles CB. **Direct sales and by mail order:** in France and abroad. Château Haut Breton Larigaudière, Soussans, 33460 Margaux.

"We have the right to show what we are capable of and to suggest that the old classifications, more than a century old, might sometimes be revised to good purpose if the opportunity and necessity were to present themselves one fine day. So let us go to visit Château Haut Breton Larigaudière; you will see what a *cru bourgeois* is and at the same time see how our harvesting is done...

Harvesting at Haut Breton Larigaudière. Drawing by Bertall. 1877.

"A victoria, drawn by a handsome horse, correctly handled, takes us in a short time up to the château halfway up the hill, surrounded by shade-giving trees. To enter the great courtyard, the carriage sweeps round in a huge circle and takes us up to the stone stairway. Straight away, a handful of charming children with dark velvety eyes and ringlets of dark brown hair forms a group round us. What a delightful sample of this lovely area! The whole range of this privileged family is present, right from the little baby, smiling in his mother's arms, to the attractive and elegant girls and the ravishing mothers and aunts who are no less beautiful... 'Welcome', says the mistress of the house graciously. 'Make yourselves at home'. 'My dear,' she says turning to her husband, 'the work force is ready: we start harvesting tomorrow.' In the morning, the harvesters, men and women alike, are ready to go. Carts drawn by sturdy horses are waiting in the side paths. Everything takes place under the vigilant eye of the men in charge and scrupulous care is observed. As in the largest châteaux, the stalks are removed and the grapes crushed in the press. The juice and the must are carried to the vats. When evening comes, the workers' plates are filled with the traditional beef soup with cabbage, prepared under the watchful eye of the mistress of the house. Then, after the evening meal, the harvesters dance to the sound of the fife and fiddle, to begin again the next day."

These extracts from *La Vigne* by Bertall (Paris 1878) depict harvesting at Haut Breton Larigaudière in a most charming and colourful manner. The proprietor, 119

M. Landau, used to take every care to ensure that his *cru* should be up to the standard of his theoretically higher-class neighbours. In 1870, Haut Breton used to produce about 30 tonneaux per year. Twenty years later, it was declaring 80, and at the beginning of the century, the quantity had dropped to 40, to finish at the end of the war at 10 and afterwards none at all in the 1960s. During the last century, the property changed hands five times. This perfectly illustrates the joys and woes of the *crus* of the Médoc which have been the subject of good or poor speculations. As from 1964, the firm of G. de Mour et Fils undertook the restoration of the vineyard on 7 hectares of its ancient soil and, since the 1980s, it has begun to show its excellent capacities for making very good wine once again. A restaurant specializing in regional gastronomy completes the visitor's enjoyment.

Hautes Graves (Château)

Commune: Soussans. **Proprietor:** Marcel Eyquem. **Size of vineyard:** 7.5 hectares. **Average age of vines:** 35 to 40 years. **Varieties:** 30% cabernet-sauvignon, 60% merlot, 10% petit-verdot. **Direct sales and by mail order:** Château Hautes Graves, Avensan, 33480 Castelnau-de-Médoc. Tel. 56 88 88 02. *It appears that this old name is making real progress after having been somewhat neglected over the last fifteen years.*

Haut-Tayac (Château)

cru bourgeois

Commune: Soussans. **Proprietor:** Christian and Viviane Saux. **Manager:** Christian Saux. **Size of vineyard:** 11 hectares. **Average age of vines:** 20 years. **Varieties:** 80% cabernet-sauvignon and cabernet-franc, 20% merlot. **Production:** 50,000 bottles CB (85% of total production). **Direct sales and by mail order:** in France and abroad. Château Haut-Tayac, Tayac, Soussans, 33460 Margaux. Tel. 56 88 34 29. **Marketing:** through the trade.

The Margaux appellation stretches along the river, and the main road which cuts through it runs from southeast to northwest, that is to say from Labarde to Tayac. This hamlet, which belongs to the commune of Soussans, was at one time greatly split up, twenty or so small proprietors owning small plots of vines here and there. Nowadays, the majority have disappeared and this gravelly plateau made up of gentle slopes rising to 40–45 feet high is consolidated into two main estates. Haut-Tayac is one of them.

Christian and Viviane Saux are the dynamic young proprietors of this vineyard of 11 hectares, whose grape varieties are entirely traditional. They came into its ownership through Viviane Saux, née Blanc, an old Soussans family which can be traced back for five generations as growers and wine producers in Tayac.

The wine of Haut-Tayac is very powerful and tannic. Slightly aggressive at first, it benefits from its time in wood and is subjected to at least one fining. Its firm constitution along with a slightly earthy flavour does not rule out that finesse to be expected from a *cru bourgeois* from Margaux.

Issan (Château d')

3e cru classé

Commune: Cantenac. **Proprietor:** SC du Château d'Issan-GFA, 33460 Margaux. Tel. 56 88 73 93. President: Madame Emmanuel Cruse. Manager: Lionel Cruse. Vineyard manager and cellar master: M. Arnaudin. **Size of vineyard:** 32 hectares. **Average age of vines:** 20 years. **Varieties:** 75% cabernet-sauvignon, 25% merlot. **Production:** 120,000 bottles CB. **Marketing:** through all the big Bordeaux wine-merchants.

In the fourteenth century, the region of Margaux was dominated by two estates, that of La Mothe-Margaux and La Mothe-Cantenac. The first has become Château Margaux and the second, Château d'Issan. These two estates greatly resemble each other by the outline of the land, their boundaries, their proximity to the river and their networks of ditches, canals and moats which formerly used to serve to transport victuals and, before that, to protect the *bastides*. So, together with Château Margaux, Château d'Issan is the oldest estate in the area and as it stands today, the château is one of the oldest in the Médoc.

In the fifteenth century, it was called Théobon, a name which is probably of Gallo-Roman origin. The estate was considerably larger than today and took in nearly the whole of the commune of Cantenac. Théobon was in the hands of different families, the Mayracs, the Ségurs, the Salignacs, the de La Vergnes, etc., until Pierre d'Essenault, a knight and a member of the Parlement de Bordeaux, took possession of it. He was responsible for demolishing the old fortified castle and, at the beginning of the seventeenth century, constructing the beautiful dwelling of today. It is from him that Issan takes its name. A century later, the Houses of Foix de Candale and Castelnau had a part interest in the seigniory and Château d'Issan. At that time, the wine of the *cru* was better known by the name of Candale. But the Revolution forced the Candales to emigrate. Their goods were confiscated and leased out to Citizen Castelnau, who preferred to let both the renown and the nobiliary particle fall into oblivion. His wife had problems with the local administration which had been set up in Margaux at that time. Their goods and chattels were sold in part at public auction, and in 1794, we find Citizen Etienne Veissière as tenant of Candale. The latter did not respect his financial obligations to the nation and all his wines were sequestrated by the Public Receiver for the national estates. At the beginning of the nineteenth century, Issan was often cited at the head of the wines of Cantenac. It belonged successively to the Dulucs (who gave their name to Château Branaire at Saint-Julien), the Blanchys and the Roys. Its classification as a 3rd *cru* in 1855 does not reflect its fine reputation over the course of the two preceding centuries. After the last war, it needed the great courage of Emmanuel Cruse to take on an estate completely overrun with weeds, a run-down vineyard, a dilapidated château and a label which, over fifty years, had reached a parlous state. With slow but steady care, his efforts succeeded in gradually restoring the estate.

All the potential was there at the outset to ensure that the *cru* could regain its former position. The 32 hectares in one practically unbroken stretch which form the vineyard have been replanted in accordance with a scheme planned to cover a twenty-year period. During this time, the buildings have been altered and the château completely restored with that slightly austere taste which fits the style of Louis XIII... and that of a Protestant outlook (the Cruses are Protestants). After the death of her husband, Madame Emmanuel Cruse brought her personal touch to the estate. Issan has become one of the important centres of the "May in Bordeaux" Festival, 121

Château d'Issan is one of the most beautiful dwellings in the Margaux appellation.

an annual and aristocratic event at which international musicians and the "crème" of whatever remains of the Bordeaux high society come together. (The programme is catholic and can include even the music of Pierre Boulez, though Count Basie is still ruled out). Her son, Lionel, took on the administration of the estate, faithfully maintaining and continuing the work begun by his father. In 1451, when the English were pursued by Dunois and driven out of the Médoc, they loaded their ships at Pauillac with all the remaining wines of Théobon. Three centuries later, the Prince

of Wales demanded that he should have wine from Candale in his cellars. Then two centuries later, the Austrian emperor, Franz-Joseph was drinking Issan as his table wine. All these were people of good taste. Issan 1900 is one of the best bottles I have ever tasted. *Regum mensis arisque deorum* (For the tables of kings and the altars of the gods) runs the motto. All the recent vintages have been successful. I am not afraid to proclaim that the former glory of Château d'Issan is still alive.

Kirwan (Château)

3e cru classé

Commune: Cantenac. **Proprietor:** Schröder & Schÿler et Cie. Manager: J.-H. Schÿler. Vineyard manager: L. Demezzo. Consultant oenologist: Monsieur Latapy. **Size of vineyard:** 34 hectares. **Average age of vines:** 18 years. **Varieties:** 40% cabernet-sauvignon, 30% merlot, 20% cabernet-franc, 10% petit-verdot. **Production:** 196,000 bottles CB. **Sales by mail order:** Château Kirwan, Cantenac, 33460 Margaux. Tel. 56 81 24 10. **Marketing:** Schröder & Schÿler et Cie, 97 quai des Chartrons, 33300 Bordeaux.

"Château Kirwan is said to be the greatest, the first of the 3rd *crus*. The fortunate proprietor of this wine-producing property extends a warm hospitality with that exquisite grace of the noble growers of Gironde and his cellars are kept perfectly."

Château Kirwan: a charming nineteenth century manor house.

In 1865, Doctor Aussel (*La Gironde à vol d'oiseau*) had several good reasons to praise Kirwan and the exquisite hospitality of Camille Godard, a refined and affable country squire who was responsible for designing the park for his château before becoming the mayor of Bordeaux. Previously he had acquired the property from a rich German wine-merchant by the name of Schryver (by pure chance of phonetics, today's proprietor is called Schÿler). The town of Bordeaux named one of its streets after the man who bequeathed it, Kirwan, in 1881, leaving his brother Adolphe Godard the tenant until his death in 1895. It was then that the highly respected firm of Schröder & Schÿler et Cie obtained the sole rights for selling the wines of Château Kirwan. In 1904, the City of Bordeaux, which knew practically nothing about viticulture, sold the estate to Daniel and Georges Guestier. The firm of Schröder and Schÿler sold the wines of Kirwan far and wide, sometimes even taking away from them the idea of *cru* and selling them as a purely commercial product without indicating their real origin or their vintage. The situation was delicate. Eros flew to the help of Hermes and Cupid to that of Mercury. For Alfred Schÿler married the daughter of Daniel Guestier. They lived happily and had many fine little Kirwans. On Daniel's death in 1924, Schröder and Schÿler bought the *cru* in order that such an unfortunate event should not reoccur.

Kirwan is a family name of Celtic origin to be found in the county of Galway in Ireland. With the intrepidity of his race, a young Kirwan married the daughter of Sir John Collingwood who in 1760 had bought the major part of the lands of Renard de La Salle (formerly, Château Kirwan was called La Salle and it was Camille Godard who brought the estate together under one wing and bought the 16 hectares featuring on the Land Register under the name of Ganet from one of the La Salle heirs). A monarchist, pro-clergy, liberal and of a fiercely Gironde character, the aristocrat Kirwan is said to have been guillotined during the Reign of Terror, leaving a large family to quarrel over the inheritance. This is probably untrue for I have found that in 1799 Marc Kirwan, then aged 64, had a certificate of residence drawn up "at Cantenac in the house belonging to him for the period September 21, 1793 to the 15th day of Nivôse in the Fourth Year of the French Republic (1796)". We learn too that he was five foot three inches tall, with blond hair and eyebrows, blue eyes, a long nose, a medium-sized mouth, a round chin, a deep forehead, an oval face and was "formerly a wine dealer in Bordeaux". A direct descendant of Jean-Henri Schÿler who founded the famous business-house with Jacques Schröder in 1739, Jean-Henri Schÿler today presides over the fate of the Société de Commerce and over Château Kirwan helped by his wife, née Christine Krug, who does not hide her Champenois origins.

The terrain of Kirwan is typical of the vast sloping plateau of Cantenac between the village and Brane. It is of dense sandy gravel in which many drains have had to be installed because the clayey subsoil lies not very deep down. But this characteristic gives very powerful concentrated wines which have at one and the same time violent tannins and a certain richness. As they age, they develop well and lose the aggressiveness of their youth. Then you can discover the traditional delicacy of Margaux wines. Each year part of the collection of casks is renewed with new oak whose subtle genuine freshness can be detected in the wine's aromatic bouquet. Particularly vulnerable in rainy years, Château Kirwan has splendid successes in great vintages, especially when the merlot which forms one-third of the vineyard is harvested in perfect condition.

Labégorce (Château)

cru bourgeois supérieur

Commune: Margaux. Proprietor: Hubert Perrodo. Technical consultant: Pierre Tari. Vineyard manager: Paul Richard. Cellar master: Michel Duboscq. Size of vineyard: 32 hectares. Average age of vines: 25 years. Varieties: 55% cabernet-sauvignon, 40% merlot, 5% cabernet-franc. Production: 190,000 bottles CB. Direct sales and by mail order: Château Labégorce, 33460 Margaux. Tel. 56 88 71 32. Marketing: through the trade. Previously, the firm CVBG in Bordeaux was the sole distributor.

Between Margaux and Soussans, Labégorce emerges from a sea of vines.

On August 31 in the year of grace 1865, Fortuné Beaucourt invested 224,000 gold francs in the purchase of Labégorce at the bar of the Court of Justice in Bordeaux. It was ten years after the classification and a century after the great frenzy for owning vines in Margaux. Arriving too late to be a *cru classé*, Fortuné Beaucourt created out of Labégorce the best *cru bourgeois supérieur* of the commune of Margaux. Previously, the affair had been complicated. My investigations have revealed that the little locality called Labégorce was "bought" in 1793 from the de Mons family, wealthy proprietors in Soussans, by Citizen Weltener who rapidly handed it onto Pierre Capelle, the latter reselling it to Signor Vastapani. Why did Vastapani call his *cru* Weltener? It is possible that there was conflict with the de Gorse widow 127 who also lived in the area. One day perhaps the stark facts of this human drama will emerge. Gorse (or Gorce) is a very old name in Guienne which spread in the Médoc during the Middle Ages (it was also the previous name of Brane-Cantenac). Over the centuries, there have been several Gorce families in Margaux and the neighbouring communes. The priest Gorce ("abbé" Gorce) probably did exist and gave his name to the place.

Fortuné Beaucourt, the new master of Labégorce carried out extensive alterations to renovate the *cru*. His strong personality and authoritative character which gained him many enemies firmly established the reputation of the wine. He was twice mayor of Margaux between 1870 and 1900 and took a keen interest in the viticultural welfare of his commune (in particular by insisting that the vines should be well drained and, to this end, he had the inhabitants clean out the ditches). He had the present château built, designed by Corcelles, the famous architect of the period. It was through his influence that the telephone first linked Bordeaux and Pauillac. In 1918, Labégorce was bought by the Rooryck family who upheld the reputation of the *cru*, but in 1965 the heirs sold out to Monsieur and Madame Robert Condom. Robert Condom was hoping to enjoy a peaceful retirement among the splendid vines on the plateau of Labégorce. He died soon after his arrival and his wife did not long survive him. Their son Jean-Robert succeeded them as owner of the *cru* but his inheritance was destined to be broken up. So Château Labégorce has just changed hands, purchased for some 100 million francs by Hubert Perrodo on his first visit; it was love at first sight. The president and owner of Techfor-Cosifor (a very large firm specializing in oil exploration), this self-taught man of 45, an indefatigable traveller, has finally found the holiday home of his dreams where he can relax... by working in a field other than that of oil. The polo matches at Giscours will enable him to practise a sport he is very keen on. And Pierre Tari is there to advise on viticulture and vinification. Hubert Perrodo will be able to allow his taste for good living to take root here. I am prepared to bet that his perfectionist approach will be quickly reflected in the quality of Labégorce's wine.

Labégorce Zédé (Château)

cru bourgeois

Communes: Soussans and Margaux. **Proprietor:** GFA Labégorce Zédé. Estate and vineyard manager: Luc Thienpont. Cellar master: Jean Bergamin. **Size of vineyard:** 26 hectares. **Average age of vines:** 25 years. **Varieties:** 50% cabernet-sauvignon, 35% merlot, 10% cabernet-franc, 5% petit-verdot. **Production:** 120,000 bottles CB. **Direct sales:** Tel. 56 88 71 31. **Marketing:** through the Bordeaux trade.

At the end of the nineteenth century, two great personalities arrived on the military scene in Europe: one came by air, Ferdinand von Zeppelin, the other by submarine, Gustave Zédé. This latter was one of the five children of Pierre Zédé, a Judge of Appeal in the Council of State and the owner of a large part of the estate of Labégorce which had been split up under the Revolution. Gustave Zédé's name has gone down in the history of naval warfare for his submersible torpedo, the *Gymnote*, created in 1888. He was the younger brother of Admiral Emile Hippolyte Zédé, who was responsible for the joint ownership of the estate called "Labégorce bis" (Labégorce No 2) up to 1891, at which date he bought out his brothers and sisters. From that time the *cru* was known by the name of Labégorce Zédé and followed an honourable path. In 1931, the Zédé heirs sold it to their former estate manager,

Labégorce-Zédé presents a fine image of a cru bourgeois.

Pierre Eyrin. Six proprietors followed one after the other up to 1961, when Jean Battesti, the former president of the Chamber of Commerce in Constantine, settled there with his family. Today, and since 1979, it is young Luc Thienpont and his wife who are in charge of the private company of Château Labégorce Zédé. Thienpont is a name of Belgian origin, well known in the wine world and in particular through its connection with Vieux-Château-Certan in Pomerol. Luc Thienpont quickly took root in this corner of Margaux territory, like a healthy petit-verdot of the best quality. He produces balanced wines which are distributed by all the major Bordeaux firms. Today, Labégorce Zédé is at the head of the Margaux *crus bourgeois*.

Labory de Tayac (Château) 🍷→ *Tayac*

Labourgade (Château de)

Commune: Arsac. **Proprietor:** Mme Texier. Consultant oenologist: Gendrot Laboratory in Bordeaux. **Size of vineyard:** 5.6 hectares. **Average age of vines:** 15 years. **Varieties:** 60% cabernet-sauvignon, 25% merlot, 15% cabernet-franc. **Production:** 6 tonneaux. **Direct sales and by mail order:** in France and abroad. Madame Texier, Château de Labourgade, Arsac, 33460 Margaux. Tel. 56 58 82 33. **Marketing:** through the trade, in bulk, returned bottled and packed. *The vines of this* cru *have recently been put back into shape and the wine can now be bought in the bottle at reasonable prices.*

La Coste (Château) 🍷

→ Paveil de Luze

La Galiane (Château)

Commune: Soussans. **Proprietors:** René and Jeanne Renon. **Size of vineyard:** 4.5 hectares. **Average age of vines:** 60 to 75 years. **Varieties:** 50% merlots, 50% cabernets. **Production:** 20,000 bottles CB. **Direct sales and by mail order:** Château La Galiane, Soussans, 33460 Margaux. Tel. 56 88 35 27.

At the time "when the English were harvesting in Aquitaine", a young and sprightly general by the name of Galian was in command of the English troops, deeply engaged in the Médoc in a hundred years war. Galian was equally at home in all the strongholds of the Médoc. But in order that the warrior should be able to rest, he needed a more comfortable nest. He created a *pied-à-terre* in Soussans in order to consecrate to Venus the free time which Mars granted him. From that moment the place passed into folklore and was long called "à Galian" (Galian's) then La Galiane, the feminine element ("la") having doubtless come about through the sentimental side of the story. Château La Galiane is the home of the Renons. It is an estate which comes to them through Madame Renon, née Miquau, but not the Miquaus from Margaux nor the Miqueaus from the Lower Médoc. No sir! The Miquaus from Soussans, who used to go twice a month to the market in Moulis in a carriage drawn by two horses. At the distant sound of their approach, everybody used to turn his back on the church of Moulis to watch them arrive. Some ten years or so ago, I lunched at La Galiane. After nibbling tasty little appetizers with an aperitif, we proceeded to a range of hors-d'oeuvre, freshly made *charcuterie,* a fish course, a delicious and rich salmi of duck, and everything washed down with the very best wines. Well after half past four in the afternoon, our stomachs were more than replete. It was at this moment that Jeanette Renon emerged from her kitchen carrying a leg of lamb of gigantic proportions surrounded by *cèpe* mushrooms. On behalf of all the guests who were begging for mercy, I said to Jeanette Renon that this was really going too far. She placed her enormous carving board on the table, put her hands on her hips and indignantly cried: "What?... Do you think I would let you leave, before the main course!..." We got up from table at seven in the evening ring after uncorking another two magnums of La Galiane 1947.

Jeanette and René Renon.

La Gombeaude (Château) 🍷→ Lascombes

La Gurgue (Château)

cru bourgeois supérieur

Commune: Margaux. **Proprietor:** Sté Bernard Taillan. Manager and director: Madame Villars. Estate manager: M. Grandchamp. Cellar master: M. Raspaud. **Size of vineyard:** 12.5 hectares. **Average age of vines:** 30 years. **Varieties:** 60% cabernet-sauvignon, 40% merlot. **Production:** 60,000 bottles CB. **Sales by mail order:** Château Chasse-Spleen, Moulis, 33480 Castelnau-de-Médoc. **Marketing:** through the trade: Hédiard, Ph. Delestrie, Duclot, Delperrier, Ginestet.

This château was one of Margaux's most highly rated "crus bourgeois supérieurs". For a long time, it was placed among the three or four *crus* just after the *crus classés* of the commune. In 1791, the banker Peixotto bought the vines of the priory of Margaux from the National Heritage and added them to his property of La Gurgue (which in the Gascon tongue should mean "little round mound").

Along with Desmirail, La Gurgue is the next-door neighbour to Château Margaux on the west side. Two former mayors of Margaux, Lanoire and Lavandier, were its owners before a private firm directed by Madame Horrière, who continued to live in the château, sold the estate in 1978 to the firm of Bernard Taillan. Excellently administered by Bernadette Villars, Château La Gurgue has made a spectacular comeback over the last five years and is among one of the best wines in Margaux.

L'Aiguillette (Clos de)

Commune: Soussans. **Proprietor:** A. Corporeau. **Size of vineyard:** 60 ares. **Average age of vines:** 40 years. **Varieties:** 33% cabernet-sauvignon, 33% merlot, 33% cabernet-franc, petit-verdot and malbec. **Marketing:** sales to private clients, friends and acquaintances. *This tiny vineyard takes its name from the narrow strip of land which fingers out to a point near Marsac. The terrain is excellent and the wine is, to all intents and purposes, not to be found.*

L'Amiral (Château de) ☖
→ *Labégorce Zédé*

Laroque (Château) ☖→ *Le Coteau*

La Rose Maucaillou (Domaine)

Commune: Soussans. **Proprietor:** Albert Maugey. **Size of vineyard:** 2 hectares. **Average age of vines:** 18 years. **Varieties:** 10% cabernet-sauvignon, 90% merlot. **Production:** 89 hectolitres. **Direct sales and by mail order:** about 6,000 bottles; M. Maugey, Château Semonlon, Avensan, 33480 Castelnau-de-Médoc. Tel. 56 58 21 29. **Marketing:** through the trade (Audy).

Albert Maugey has a larger property in Avensan where he makes the wines of Château Semonlon with the "Haut-Médoc" appellation. In Soussans, he makes wines of good quality.

Larruau (Château)

Commune: Margaux. **Proprietor:** Bernard Chateau. **Size of vineyard:** 4 hectares. **Average age of vines:** 15 years. **Varieties:** 2/3 cabernet-sauvignon, 1/3 merlot. **Production:** 12,000 bottles CB. **Direct sales and by mail order:** Château Larruau, 4 rue de La Trémoïlle, 33460 Margaux. Tel. 56 88 35 50. **Marketing:** through the trade.

Augustin Dubignon-Talbot was the rates' assessor for the Margaux region in Year IV of the Republic (1796). Château Dubignon-Talbot was a 3rd *cru classé* in the official classification of 1855. With the death of Augustin, two new *crus* by the name of Dubignon were born, one called Philippe, and the other G. Martial, later Marcellin. In about 1865, the Fourcade family added Philippe Dubignon to the vineyards of Saint-Exupéry, Malescot, La Colonie, Prévôt de Lacroix. At the end of the nineteenth century, Malescot-Saint-Exupéry, 3rd *cru classé* (Dubignon included) was the largest vineyard in Margaux after Château Margaux itself.

During this time, Monsieur Veron-Réville lived in Château Dubignon-Talbot and from what vines remained, he produced five to eight tonneaux of wine a year. In 1904, Pierre Mellet bought the micro-estate and increased production to more than twenty tonneaux. In 1960, the name disappeared, for Jean Cordier, the proprietor of Château Talbot at Saint-Julien, bought the vines up, only to sell them again to Château Margaux and Malescot. Third-class Dubignon-Talbot had a third-class burial. Since that time, young Bernard Chateau has recreated a vineyard of four

Bernard Chateau in his vineyard.

hectares and produced a label with the name of Larruau, an area of the village of Margaux which was the site of the old château Dubignon-Talbot. It is one of the most charming houses in the village. Generally speaking, the wine of Château Larruau produced by Bernard Chateau is quite exceptional. The vineyard is only fifteen years old, but on tasting the wine you would say that it is at least twice that age. My admiration for Bernard Chateau and his wine never ceases. I consider it to be the best value for money in Margaux. The fact of maturing in wood gives it a close resemblance to the great *crus classés*.

Lascombes (Château)

2e cru classé

Commune: Margaux. **Proprietor:** Sté viticole du Château Lascombes belongs to the firm of Lichine, part of the English Bass-Charrington group. Director: Alain Maurel. Manager: René Vannetelle. Estate Manager: Claude Gobinau. Cellar master: Serge Ladra. Vineyard manager: Jean-Pierre Sougnoux. **Size of vineyard:** 94 hectares. **Average age of vines:** between 5 and 30 years. **Varieties:** 65% cabernet, 33% merlot, 2% petit-verdot. **Production:** about 300,000 bottles of "grand vin" CB. **Direct sales and by mail order:** Sté du Château Lascombes, 33460 Margaux. Tel. 56 88 70 66. **Marketing:** through the trade; Alexis Lichine et Cie, 109 rue Achard, 33300 Bordeaux.

As from the fifties, the late Alexis Lichine focused the interest of American wine lovers on the wines of France and, in particular, on the great *crus* of Bordeaux. A tireless traveller, a man with a golden tongue, persuasive, blessed with good taste, he breathed new life into the Médoc and Margaux was the first to benefit from 133 this polished entrepreneur. Not content merely with attracting the attention of the Press, importers and distributors, he made himself known to the rich families of New York, New England and California, teaching them how to start a cellar, and how to serve and drink wines, all according to the rules of the art; in short, how to marry great wines to their public and private social standing. When he persuaded David Rockefeller to spend some time in Margaux and to visit Château Lascombes with a view to becoming a shareholder, Rockefeller asked Pierre Ginestet's advice and was told "Being a shareholder in a vineyard will not greatly enrich you, but it is one of the rare investments whose dividends you will always be able to savour." So in 1952, led by the pilgrim Alexis Lichine, a group of wealthy Americans bought Château Lascombes. This was the start of the extraordinary drama of the man who was to become the "High Pontiff of Wine".

In the beginning, Lascombes (which owes its name to the Chevalier de Lascombes, born in 1625) was linked to the firm of Durfort-Duras. Classed among the 2nd *crus* in 1855, it belonged to the president of the Bar, Chaix d'Est-Ange, at the end of the last century. It was the latter who under Napoleon III upheld the cause of France against Egypt at the time of the lawsuit over the Suez Canal. The château of today with its Anglo-baroque appearance and unfinished look dates from this period. On the death of Chaix d'Est-Ange, the vineyard was split up into a thousand pieces which were gleaned by neighbouring *crus*. My grandfather and my father partly restored it during the twenties, then sold it to a limited company who did little for its reputation. During the last war, it was the secret office of the Canadian General Brutinel, the Head of Intelligence for the Allied Armies for southwest France and Spain. A great strategist, General Brutinel had predicted the invasion of June 1944 two years in advance. Thanks to the drive of Alexis Lichine, Lascombes speeded up its programme of reorganization to the extent of increasing the production tenfold over twenty years. Today, the cellars, enlarged several times over, are some of the largest in the Margaux appellation.

In 1971, Château Lascombes was sold to the English brewers, Bass-Charrington, which already owned Alexis Lichine's business in Bordeaux, whose president, Alain Maurel, came from an old Bordeaux family. Unfortunately, he passed away in

Lascombes is one of the most visited crus *in the Margaux appellation...*

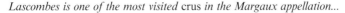

...and its cellar, one of the most majestic.

November 1989 and his death is causing some trouble in the management of the company.

Lascombes's skills are thoroughly up to date but it offers time-honoured hospitality. A vat-house inaugurated for the 1986 harvest placed modern techniques at the service of Médoc traditions. The visitor cannot but be impressed by this series of 32 stainless-steel vats situated on the first floor, so enabling them to be emptied by the force of gravity, as in former days. It is also interesting to be able to observe at one and the same time practices of yesterday and today: those of yesterday, when men and women standing over a conveyor belt hand-select the grapes picked by 200 harvesters; those of today, when the cellar master calls into play the electronic system to regulate the temperature of each of the fermentation vats.

Along with this aim for perfection should be mentioned the new Château Segonnes. This *cru bourgeois*, inspired by the house next to the château, is Château Lascombes's second wine.

The proprietors also know how to welcome visitors. The Hollywood-style swimming-pool holds pride of place and there are more than a hectare of trees, rhododendrons and English lawns separating the Château's extensive car park – a veritable haven of peace in the heart of this Margaux vineyard.

None the less, thanks to Alexis Lichine and his friends and thanks to the powerful British firm which now owns it, Château Lascombes is a fine estate which does honour to the commune of Margaux and its soil. A large reception room next to the cellars housing the latest vintage regularly welcomes the many groups which come from all over the world. I leave Alexis Lichine to describe the characteristics of his one-time protégé: "Château Lascombes excels in finesse. It has a light indefinable bouquet which underlines the feminine qualities of the wines of the Médoc and which, to some, is evocative of violets. It matures quite quickly but is none the less a wine with a long life in front of it" (*Encyclopaedia of Wines and Spirits*, Weidenfeld & Nicolson, 1979).

La Tour de Bessan (Château)

Commune: Soussans. **Proprietor:** Lucien Lurton. Cellar master: M. Birot. **Size of vineyard:** 21 hectares. **Average age of vines:** 15 years. **Varieties:** 90% cabernet-sauvignon, 10% merlot. **Production:** 80,000 to 100,000 bottles CB. **Marketing:** through the trade; Société de Distribution des Vins Fins, Z.I. de la Mouline, 33560 Carbon-Blanc.

The "tower" of Bessan still exists, near the brook called La Louise in the commune of Soussans. In the fifteenth century, it was one of the many watch-towers which the English had built all over the Médoc to keep a look out over the territory. After the reign of Charles VII, it was of no further use and served as a climbing frame for ivy, a nesting place for birds, a hiding place for poachers, and a trysting-place for lovers who over the centuries have covered its walls with amorous epitaphs and other doubtful declarations. As for the "château", it has never existed as a building, but we know that in Bordeaux (just as in Spain) châteaux can exist in the imagination. And it is with this entrepreneurial imagination that Lucien Lurton created a vineyard with the name of La Tour de Bessan. This new name felicitously increases the number of his many labels for his large production of Margaux AOC. Until relatively recently, La Tour de Bessan was used to describe the wines from the loamy soil of Château La Tour-de-Mons. La Tour de Bessan gives light, slightly fruity wines which enable the names of Margaux and Lurton to be linked together without costing too much.

La Tour-de-Mons (Château)

cru bourgeois supérieur

Commune: Soussans. **Proprietor:** Family trust: Clauzel-Cruchet. Director and estate manager: Bertrand Clauzel. Vineyard manager and cellar master: Christian Clauzel. **Size of vineyard:** 30 hectares. **Average age of vines:** 25 years. **Varieties:** 45% cabernet-sauvignon, 40% merlot, 10% cabernet-franc, 5% petit-verdot. **Production:** 150,000 bottles CB. **Direct sales and by mail order:** in France. Château La Tour-de-Mons, Soussans, 33460 Margaux. Tel. 56 88 33 03. **Marketing:** through the Bordeaux trade.

Two centuries before Christopher Columbus discovered America, Jehan de Colomb discovered the Médoc and decided to settle there. That took place in 1289 in Soussans. This was the period of Bordeaux's first great economic boom, helped by the presence of the English who encouraged the well-to-do people of the city to develop viticulture in Guienne. The great families of the time were the Bégueys, the Monadeys, the Salters, the Colombs. Thus it was a Colomb who built La Tour-de-Mons. This historic house, the oldest in the area, has undergone structural alterations several times, but it has resisted the passing of time and its foundations are still those of the thirteenth century. This estate, the vineyard and its château are entirely authentic Margaux antiquities. Up to the Revolution, La Tour-de-Mons was the largest "house" in Soussans. You could say that this estate is rather a special

Bertrand Clauzel at La Tour de Mons.

case, for it has survived inheritances or marriages, remaining unscathed, with the single exception that at the end of the *ancien régime,* the emigration of part of the de Mons family reduced by more than three-quarters the size of the estate, which used to stretch unbroken from Bessan to Labégorce. The most recent people to come into the *cru* are represented by the Clauzel-Cruchet joint family trust. The estate is administered by Bertrand Clauzel, the former mayor of Soussans, and his son Christian, a born viticulturalist. Grandfather Dubos was an outstanding vintner.

CHATEAU
LA TOUR DE MONS
MARGAUX

At Cantemerle and La Tour-de-Mons, he produced some remarkable wines which tasters of long ago still remember with a tear in their eye. I can recall a blind tasting of the 1953s, in which La Tour-de-Mons had been surreptitiously slipped into the midst of twelve or so *crus classés*. It held its own against them all. Its richness and depth were such that no one knew quite what it was or how to place it. In point of fact, the wines of La Tour-de-Mons have an individual special personality which distinguishes them from the majority of Margaux wines. They can often be taken for Pauillacs and, formerly, for wines from Pomerol or Graves. But the majority of the time, they give the wine lover tremendous pleasure when he tastes them. Their sale price is more or less on a par with that of the *crus classés*, a fact justified by the fidelity of their customers.

La Tourelle (Clos de) ♟

→ *Monbrison*

Le Coteau (Château)

Commune: Arsac. **Proprietor:** M. and Madame Claude Léglise. Consultant oenologist: M. Gendrot. **Size of vineyard:** 6 hectares. **Average age of vines:** 25 years. **Varieties:** 75% cabernet-sauvignon, 20% merlot, 5% cabernet-franc and petit-verdot. **Production:** 35 tonneaux, 40,000 bottles CB. **Direct Sales:** Tel. 56 58 82 30, **and by mail order:** in France and abroad: M. and Madame Claude Léglise, Le Coteau, Arsac, 33460 Margaux. **Marketing:** through the trade.

Les Alouettes (Clos)

Commune: Arsac. **Proprietor:** André Micas, 8 rue Maurice Fillon, Parempuyre, 33290 Blanquefort. Tel. 56 57 00 42. **Size of vineyard:** 2,256 vines. **Average age of vines:** 10 to 15 years. **Varieties:** 850 cabernet-sauvignon, 350 merlot, 200 malbec, 100 muscat. *Les Alouettes is undoubtedly the quaintest of all Margaux wines and the hardest to find too, for it is "unsellable" — which is just how its proprietor wants it to be.*

Les Baraillots (Château)

Commune: Margaux. **Proprietor:** Michel Brunet. **Size of vineyard:** 4.80 hectares. **Average age of vines:** 20 years. **Varieties:** cabernet, merlot, petit-verdot. **Production:** 25,000 bottles CB. **Direct sales and by mail order:** Château Les Baraillots, 2-4 rue Corneillan, 33460 Margaux. Tel. 56 88 33 56 or 56 88 74 19. **Marketing:** through the trade for a part of the production.

Michel Brunet and his family live on their estate of 24 hectares of which one-fifth is under vines. The rest is given over to livestock. The vineyard, consisting of two main parcels, was separated from Palmer and Durfort in 1928 and 1933. It is of good permeable gravelly soil which can be worked in the most traditional way. Vinification and ageing conform to classical procedures. All this is conscientious.

Michel Brunet is totally devoted to his estate, one of the rare 'crus artisans' in the Margaux appellation.

In the Médoc dialect, "barrail" or "barralhe" means an enclosure or, more often, a slight bank of earth marking out a boundary between two fields or serving as a dyke along a ditch. The little "barrails" of Château Les Baraillots mark out its territory in relation to the surrounding *crus classés*. It is one of the very rare *crus artisans* from Margaux as such. The wine is firm, full of tannin and very sappy. It is a pity that it is almost always sold and drunk too soon.

Les Graves du Soc (Château) ♟ ♟ ♟ ♟ ♟

Commune: Arsac. **Proprietor:** Jacques and Jean-Paul Bosc. **Size of vineyard:** 1.67 hectares. **Average age of vines:** 20 years. **Varieties:** 20% merlot, 70% cabernet-sauvignon, 10% cabernet-franc. **Production:** 10 to 11 tonneaux. **Direct sales:** projected. Jean-Paul Bosc, Le Sablot, Arsac, 33460 Margaux. Tel. 56 58 82 20. **Marketing:** through the trade.

The commune of Arsac has seen its population quadruple in fifteen years. A large part of it has been taken up by housing estates. Not only did the number of vines markedly decrease after the First World War, but the gravel diggers made a part of the gravelly plateaux look like Gruyère cheese. There is a considerable area covered with forests of pines and coppices of oak trees which protect the vines from the Atlantic salt winds. For just a generation vines have been cultivated again between five houses and two gravel quarries. Jacques Bosc, Jean-Paul's father is from an old Arsac family. Staunchly opposing the gravel quarries and housing estates, he has been able to protect his small vineyard. Part lies at Carabin in the middle of large châteaux and part is in "au Gravier" on fine slopes of the Margaux appellation. It is a great pity that the care given to cultivation and vinification is not rewarded by château bottling. But I hear that it is under experiment and a label has already been created. Well done.

Les Gravières (Château) 🏠→ Tayac

Les Vimières le Tronquéra (Château) ♟ ♟ ♟ ♟ ♟

Commune: Soussans. **Proprietors:** M. and Madame Jacques Boissenot. **Size of vineyard:** 0.46 hectares. **Average age of vines:** 45 years. **Varieties:** 20% cabernet-sauvignon, 80% merlot. **Production:** 2 tonneaux, 2,500 bottles CB. **Visits:** M. Boissenot, tel. 56 58 91 74. **Direct sales and by mail order:** in France. M. and Madame Jacques Boissenot, 47 rue Principale, Lamarque, 33460 Margaux.

Just like a maritime pilot who has his pleasure boat, Jacques Boissenot bought this little vineyard of less than half a hectare in 1984. So he can put into practice the advice he gives his clients. For Jacques Boissenot, a star pupil of Prof. Emile Peynaud, is an oenologist, well known in the Médoc and in love with his profession. He has succeeded the master as consultant oenologist at Château Lafite-Rothschild. 139

He has no difficulty in slipping the slim production of his micro-château among the circle of his friends and acquaintances. You can always try and edge your way in; you will find concentrated wines, supple and powerful, forcefully expressing the dominating influence of the merlot.

Ligondras (Château)

Commune: Arsac. **Proprietor:** Pierre Augeau. Consultant oenologist: M. Duval-Arnaud from the Gendrot Laboratory in Bordeaux. **Size of vineyard:** 8.30 hectares. **Average age of vines:** 30 years. **Varieties:** 70% cabernet, 30% merlot. **Production:** 35,000 to 45,000 bottles CB. **Visits:** by appointment for groups, tel. 56 58 80 98. **Direct sales and by mail order:** in France and abroad. Château Ligondras, Arsac, 33460 Margaux. **Marketing:** through the trade.

Traditional Bordeaux casks at Ligondras.

This is a fine plateau of sandy, gravelly soil in the commune of Arsac, halfway between the village and Brane. The predominant variety is the cabernet. It gives a firm wine rich in body and colour which fills the mouth and which loses none of these characteristics when it is left to age. Pierre Augeau inherited this property from his father. Formerly, it belonged to Château Vincent at Issan, Cantenac. The house attached to Château Ligondras is typical of those constructed in the Médoc at the end of the last century, despite the recent improvements which create a certain lack of architectural harmony. You will always be warmly welcomed at Ligondras. If the proprietor is not at home, you will have to look for him in the vineyard or in the cellar, for he keeps an eye on everything.

Loyac (Château) 🛈
→ Malescot Saint-Exupéry

Malescot Saint-Exupéry (Château)

3e cru classé

Commune: Margaux. **Proprietor:** Roger Zuger. Vineyard manager: Jean-Claude Durand. Cellar master: Jean-François Miquau. **Size of vineyard:** 34 hectares. **Average age of vines:** 35 years. **Varieties:** 50% cabernet-sauvignon, 35% merlot, 10% cabernet-franc, 5% petit-verdot. **Production:** 180,000 bottles CB. **Direct sales and by mail order:** in France. Château Malescot Saint-Exupéry, 33460 Margaux. Tel. 56 88 70 68. **Marketing:** through the trade; "sole rights" distributors in each country.

Following his father, and my own, Roger Zuger is the president of the Viticultural Federation of the Margaux Appellation which succeeds the Federation of Margaux Vineyards, created in 1920, when Margaux was not an AOC. At that time, Malescot Saint-Exupéry was the property of the English firm of W. H. Chaplin & Co. Limited, who specialized in importing Australian wines. But since the beginning of the nineteenth century, Malescot is one of the *crus* in the Médoc which has changed hands the most often. In 1827, Count Jean-Baptiste de Saint-Exupéry added his name to that of Malescot (he was prosecutor at the Parlement de Bordeaux in the seventeenth century). At the same time, he added a number of surrounding vines such as those of La Colonie and Loyac. Fourcade, who succeeded him as from 1853, continued this form of voracity by swallowing up Dubignon (Philippe), Prévôt de Lacroix, and various other different parcels round about. This is what is still today archly called "judicious exchanges"... From 1850 to 1865, the production of Malescot Saint-Exupéry rose from 75 to 200 tonneaux. In ten years, 500,000 vines were planted. The task of ploughing and working the vines was carried out by fourteen oxen and six horses. Harvesting needed a work-force of an army of nearly three hundred people.

Ten proprietors followed one after the other in less than a hundred and fifty years, then Château Malescot Saint-Exupéry was finally bought by Paul Zuger on June 1, 1955. The imposing estate had been reduced to seven hectares of ailing vines, dilapidated buildings, worn-out equipment and a run-down reputation. In thirty years, Paul Zuger and his son Roger have restored the vineyard to dimensions 141

Roger and Nicole Zuger have given new life to Malescot Saint-Exupéry.

commensurate with those of a *cru classé*. The roofs have been repaired, the cellars re-equipped and a new building for bottling, packing and storing has been completed. Passionately keen on heraldry and as hungry for coats of arms as Billy Bunter for buns, Roger Zuger has had the coat of arms of the Count of Saint-Exupéry on Malescot's label reprinted in fine leaf-gold with two lions rampant, one on either side of the escutcheon, their feet holding down the banner whereon we read the proud and noble family motto *Semper ad altum*.

Château Malescot Saint-Exupéry is a remarkable example of the vicissitudes through which a *cru* can pass and its transient moments of glory from one century to another. A parallel could be made between the caprices of the climate of the Médoc and those of the fate of its *grands crus*. In the same way, we could also pass judgement on the 1855 classification which established five groups of privileged châteaux, of which certain ones have since shown themselves worthy, either temporarily or permanently, and others have completely disappeared. In the preface of his *Richesses gastronomiques de France, les vins de Bordeaux,* Charles de Lorbac wrote: "Large plantations (large, depending on whether or not they were created with discernment), different ways of making wine, and many other factors can in the long run modify the quality of an estate's wine. But apart from the rôle played by man's initiative, it must be admitted that nature plays the largest part, and that if there are only a certain number of privileged *crus*, this is because of the predominating influence of the soil and subsoil, often even because of a few mysterious secrets of nature, something intangible, unknown, which has led people to say that Margaux, for example, was a 'stroke of luck!' "

Malescot's vineyard today is spread out over five areas in Margaux and Soussans. The oldest parcels are contiguous with Château Margaux on typical gravelly slopes with complementary densities, generally well exposed. Vinification is done in "the old style" with a fermentation period of thirty days. The evolution of the wine as it ages is slow, but the aromas change from year to year, changes worthy of a dazzling kaleidoscope. The initial raspberry aroma of the new wine turns into blackberry and blackcurrant, changing yet again later to a bouquet of violets.

Margaux (Château)

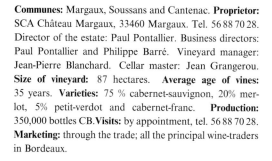

1er cru classé

Communes: Margaux, Soussans and Cantenac. **Proprietor:**
SCA Château Margaux, 33460 Margaux. Tel. 56 88 70 28.
Director of the estate: Paul Pontallier. Business directors:
Paul Pontallier and Philippe Barré. Vineyard manager:
Jean-Pierre Blanchard. Cellar master: Jean Grangerou.
Size of vineyard: 87 hectares. **Average age of vines:**
35 years. **Varieties:** 75 % cabernet-sauvignon, 20% mer-
lot, 5% petit-verdot and cabernet-franc. **Production:**
350,000 bottles CB.**Visits:** by appointment, tel. 56 88 70 28.
Marketing: through the trade; all the principal wine-traders
in Bordeaux.

The Very Important Official close to the President of the Fifth French Republic
removed his spectacles and raised his eyes to the Louis XV chandelier round which
the flies were circling. "But my dear Sir, you must understand that to allow Château
Margaux to be bought by Americans is as if we were to agree to sell them the Eiffel
Tower or the Gioconda." I protested that there was little in common between the
Eiffel Tower and a field of merlot, and that the Mona Lisa was an imported work
of art which anybody could hang anywhere. He paid no attention. "And again, you
must realize, my dear Sir, that we cannot go against the wishes of the President of the
Republic who has given a clear ruling on this matter. Margaux will remain French.
Do you realize that the Americans have actually refused permission for Concorde
to land on their soil?" This is how the National Distillers Company was prevented
from buying Château Margaux, just when my father and I thought to have found
a suitable taker, whose humanitarian, technical, commercial and financial structure
was of international proportions, a taker who would be what the Rothschilds are to
Lafite and Mouton. For nearly two years, the sale of Château Margaux had been a
major matter of state which had received press coverage out of all proportion. The
following two blank lines represent everything I have to say, or rather not to say,
on this subject:
"

".

Finally, the "French Solution" so much sought after by the government was found
thanks to André Mentzelopoulos, the president of the firm of Félix Potin. Here I recall with admiration this man of exceptional qualities, a formidable negotiator and
a man of dazzling intelligence. Nicholas Faith's book, entitled *Château Margaux*
traces the history of the estate. First published by Nathan Press in 1981, it has been
most elegantly re-edited by Flammarion, enriched with magnificent photographs by
Michel Guillard. Everyone tells his own story in his own way. Here then is mine:
In the thirteenth century, the land of La Mothe belonged to the Albret family.
Several authors state that for a time it was owned by Edward II, King of England.
As from the fifteenth century, the lineage of the barons of La Mothe-Margaux is
well known. We find the names of Montferrand, Durfort, Gimel, Lory, Lestonnac,
Aulède, Fumel, Hargicourt... More often than not, the seigniory of La Mothe,
which (like the majority of the estates of the region) was under the control of Blanquefort, was handed on through matrimonial alliances. It was at the very beginning
of the eighteenth century that the idea of *cru* first appeared, resulting in the nascent
supremacy of the vineyards of Margaux, Lafite, Latour and Pontac (Haut-Brion),
established by the position they occupied in all the courts of Europe and more especially with the English aristocracy. The great pioneers of this viticultural revolution 143

The façade of Château Margaux is world famous.

were the Aulèdes, the Fumels, the Ségurs and the Pontacs who established great vineyards and then substituted the appellation of the estate for that of the parish from which the wines came.

Topographically speaking, the respective situations of each of the three great *crus* (the first ones in the Médoc) are comparable in every particular (Issan and Beychevelle can also be included with them in this respect). The château and working buildings are constructed on the eastern limit of the pebbly stretch beside the low-lying area of loamy soils. The vineyards lie on slopes stretching out towards the river, and the composition of their gravels is varied yet complementary. At

Château Margaux, the brook of Le Lestonnat, fed by the channel of the Aubion, flows into the west side of the fishpond. The network of the park's watercourses has been developed for aesthetic reasons, but originally it was created to ensure that the pebbly slopes under vines were well drained. The geomorphology of the soil lent itself more readily than anywhere else to this project. In the Middle Ages and up to the seventeenth century, the canals which linked the moats of the château to the river were navigable at high tide. For centuries, long narrow boats which were called *aguilas* (needles) because of their shape preceded the barges which were still in use fifty years ago. They circulated between Margaux and Bordeaux, Bourg, 145

Blaye, Mortagne and Pauillac, furthering trade and ensuring the transport of casks of wine: "In Bordeaux, having taken on board a large number of tonneaux and casks of wine, the boats used to take on a further cargo at Macau, the Bec-d'Ambès, Margaux and other points in the Médoc" (Francisque Michel, *Histoire du commerce et de la navigation à Bordeaux,* Bordeaux 1867). Despatched directly to England, Holland or other destinations, the wines did not suffer the excessive transport costs and the tolls levied in Bordeaux.

The vineyard of La Mothe-Margaux owes its exceptional quality to the economic opportunity offered by its geographical conditions. All these natural conditions combined to make one of the best viticultural terrains in the world. The perfectionist efforts of great families have done the rest and it is thanks to an initial conjuncture of good fortune, favourable circumstances and coordinated efforts that Château Margaux is now in a class of its own.

Towards the end of the seventeenth century, Margaux was in the hands of the Aulède family from Lestonnac. An estate manager by the name of Berlon brought his ingenuity and personality to bear, much to the benefit of the *cru*. Professor René Pijassou ranks him with Dom Pérignon for his many innovations in the field of vinification. He was one of the first to separate the white grapes from the black, when traditionally every vineyard was composed of between a fifth and a tenth of white grapes (even forty years ago, sémillon and white merlot were to be found among the cabernet and merlot). In the eighteenth century, François d'Aulède died without any direct descendant and his sister Catherine became the Lady of Margaux. She ran her estate like a Lord before leaving it to her son Louis, who had only the time to hand it onto Joseph, his youngest child. The latter had an only daughter, Louise who, traumatized by this disgrace which Nature had imposed upon her and the victim of an ageing Louis XV, married Jean-Baptiste du Barry, the brother of the infamous countess and mistress of the king's bed-chamber. Finding this name embarrassing, Jean-Baptiste du Barry, having tried in vain to appropriate the escutcheon of his father-in-law, Fumel, finally took that of his mother-in-law, née Conte d'Hargicourt.

In 1789, several days after the storming of the Bastille, Count d'Hargicourt packed his bags and crossed the Pyrenees. His wife and ageing father-in-law stayed behind to face the harsh realities of the Revolution. Margaux was confiscated lock, stock and tonneau. A local farmer, called Miqueau, was nominated to complete this pillage. It was at that time, about 1795, that Laure de Fumel, the last of her line, bought the estate with her own means, marrying at the same time Count Hector Brane, who gave her a son before fleeing to Germany. In less than no time, she married a certain Langsdorff who was in the import-export business. Oppressive taxation, a host of conflicting interests and a string of debts led her to unload her property to a certain Marquis de La Colonilla, whose real name was Bertrand Douat. A lengthy and vitriolic lawsuit followed. Several years of litigation were needed for the marquis to bring his legal and financial problems to a conclusion.

In 1810, Douat de La Colonilla turned the page and commissioned a new château from Emile Combes, the architect who was a pupil of Victor Louis. We have no picture of the former château which must have looked like one of the many *bastides* in Guienne. Nor do we know its exact site. Judging by the layout of the land,

Racking is carried out in the most traditional way.

it could well have been on the site of the present cellars or in the old park. Six years later, all the working buildings, the château and the workers' living quarters were reconstructed. Douat de La Colonilla died. The property was more or less abandoned for a period of twenty years until his three children sold it to the wealthy banker Aguado, a true Castilian. A great financier, a dandy and a patron of the arts, Count Aguado, the Marquis of Las Marismas, was one of the outstanding figures of the romantic Paris of that time. His wife kept one of the most brilliant salons in the capital. He died in 1842 and his eldest son, Alexandre, accompanied by his beautiful wife Emily, modelled his behaviour on that of his father. But stricken with madness, he died young. Emily married his handsome young brother, Viscount Onoesippe (or Onésime), and became a lady-in-waiting to the Empress Eugénie, of

A subterranean cellar has been built for wines in their second year.

whom she was a childhood friend and whom she followed into exile in England. When she became the widow of her second Aguado, she sold Margaux in 1879 to Count Pillet-Will, the governor of the Bank of France. He brought his personal kudos to the name of Château Margaux, giving it his own name and his family coat of arms. But he was scarcely repaid, for he came to the vineyards of the Médoc at the time of an intense economic crisis which had been heightened by

the invasion of phylloxera and the propagation of mildew. Striving for quality and concerned for his reputation and that of his wine, he sold all his vintages in two lots called "1st wine" and "2nd wine". The term "Grand Vin" (Great Wine), which we find on almost all the labels of Bordeaux and elsewhere, had no other meaning, originally, than to indicate this qualitative selection. In order to distinguish clearly between the "Great" and the "Second" wines, Pillet-Will created a second label, the 149

Pavillon Rouge of Château Margaux, equivalent to the Pavillon Blanc which was the name of the traditional but small production of white wines, mainly destined for the personal consumption of the proprietors. The Duke de La Trémoïlle, the son-in-law of Pillet-Will, ran the estate on the death of the latter in 1911. He sold it ten years later to a limited company which my family joined in 1934.

When my father became the director of Château Margaux, there were five vintages remaining unsold in the cellars, only a third of the vineyard had been well looked after and was in good condition, and the staff had not been paid for six months. He worked like a Trojan, uprooting and replanting the most run-down areas of vines, improving the exhausted land, exchanging other parcels with neighbouring vineyards in order to restore some kind of unity to the estate. After the war in 1949, my grandfather Fernand Ginestet and my father managed to buy the rest of the shares in the firm from the Boylandry and Lurton families. My own family then had the courage to go and live in the château which the German troops had ransacked. My mother undertook the renovation of the château and the gardens. It was she who brought warmth and life to the cold austerity of this great house. During the fifties and the sixties my family was the only proprietor of a *premier cru classé* actually living on the estate. The death of my brother Jean-François and the collapse of the Bordeaux wine market in the early seventies compelled us to find a "happy end". As suggested above, the rôle played by the French government in this affair has not been very helpful. On March 23, 1977, the sale contract was signed between the new firm of Château Margaux (created by André Mentzelopoulos under the aegis of Félix Potin) and the Ginestets.

Discovering a world which up to then was unknown to him, André Mentzelopoulos threw himself wholeheartedly into running his new investment in real and landed estate (he never benefited from this for he died after the 1980 harvest). He brought to Margaux a host of first-class specialists, determined to justify their fees by recommending sweeping changes. While the cultivation and oenological specialists were looking after the vineyard and cellars, the architects, decorators, antique dealers and landscape gardeners were attending to the château and its surroundings. So Château Margaux changed. I refrain from making judgement on the new look, while respectfully admiring (from a distance) the power of Mammon. But I think that these transformations were carried out with dazzling rapidity. The family atmosphere and spirit of human understanding in which Château Margaux used to be run has given way to an institutional rigidity with its carefully calculated demands. The result should give an irreproachable quality and here, I acknowledge that this has indeed been the case for the last few vintages. Château Margaux has doubtless had, once more in its history, the good luck to meet Dame Fortune. From now on, it is incontestably the greatest.

Marquis d'Alesme-Becker (Château)

3e cru classé

Communes: Soussans and Margaux. **Proprietor:** Jean-Claude Zuger, who runs the estate helped by his cellar master, André Pelletan. **Size of vineyard:** about 10 hectares. **Average age of vines:** 25 years. **Varieties:** 30% cabernet-sauvignon, 30% merlot, 30% cabernet-franc, 10% petit-verdot. **Production:** 60,000 bottles CB. **Direct sales and by mail order:** in France. Château Marquis d'Alesme, 33460 Margaux. Tel. 56 88 70 27. **Marketing:** in foreign countries, sales by direct importers, without intervention of local business.

Château Desmirail, today Château Marquis d'Alesme-Becker.

After many changes of character, the Marquis d'Alesme has finally found and asserted its identity. Once upon a time in the charming little village of Margaux there lived a likeable marquis called d'Alesme. In this region, blessed by the gods, he owned a vineyard, not large but well kept, which gave good ripe grapes from which he made an exquisite wine. That was a very long time ago, about the beginning of the seventeenth century. Two hundred years later, a connoisseur called Becker (or Bekker) while strolling through the vineyards of the lords of Margaux, discovered by chance this little lonesome orphaned spot and he decided on the spot to adopt it. The child was acknowledged by true amateurs and was thereafter called Marquis d'Alesme-Becker. Without increasing its small stature, it slipped in among the 3rd *crus classés* at the time of the 1855 revision. That passed unnoticed. But its new father, Sznajderski, was delighted. Then the wicked Arthur de Gassowski took advantage of Sznajderski's old age to buy the estate but sold it again at the end of the century to Monsieur Chaix d'Est-Ange who put it to bed with Lascombes. Wishing to avenge the Hundred Years War, some English people, who had succeeded in hoisting the Union Jack at Malescot Saint-Exupéry, bought the Marquis d'Alesme-Becker from Chaix d'Est-Ange's son. But as all this was difficult to pronounce, Messrs W. H. Chaplin & Co. Ltd., in a spirit of distillation of which only they held the secret, called the whole shooting-match Malescot. They even transformed this name into "Male Scot" to give a dash of local Scottish colour. The ladies of London society went into raptures: *Please, give me a kilt of male Scot!*

In 1938, an engineer of the Zuger Mines in Alsace became concerned about the province's security. He came to Margaux and bought Château Desmirail, to which his beautiful daughter brought the name Ritz. Desmirail and Marquis d'Alesme had disappeared as *crus*. It is now that a good fairy appeared and announced: "The Marquis d'Alesme-Becker will find a château and it shall be that of Desmirail. The label of Desmirail will have its own wine and it shall be that of Lucien Lurton." All that happened in less time than it takes to write it. In 1969, the situation was so far from being clear that Féret in his re-styled and enlarged twelfth edition of *Bordeaux et ses vins* published on one page a photo of a beautiful Louis XIII château, 151 under the heading of "Château Marquis d'Alesme-Becker, 3rd *cru classé*", and on the page opposite, an old engraving of the same château under the heading of "Château Desmirail, 3rd *cru classé*". And yet, in 1966 a label had been printed to commemorate the 350th anniversary of the "name".

The Marquis d'Alesme-Becker is in the hands of Jean-Claude Zuger, who is the son of Paul and brother of Roger (*see* Malescot Saint-Exupéry). He recreated a vineyard in 1977, broke away from the family business in 1979 and had an independent vat-house and cellars constructed. Since then, and not without pride, he has his name printed on the label with its equestrian motif and featuring the coronet of the Marquis d'Alesme. Will the horseshoe in which the name of the château is inscribed bring good luck? One step further and we shall have "Marquis d'Alesme-Zuger". And why not, for heaven's sake? We have seen many other even stranger changes in the Médoc, this ancient land of spells and wizardry. Jean-Claude Zuger is a local man and he makes good wine which has the good fortune to be a 3rd *cru classé*.

At the end of a well-prepared restoration, Marquis de Terme's renovated buildings.

Marquis de Terme (Château)

ŸŸŸŸ♈

4e cru classé

Commune: Margaux. **Proprietor:** Pierre-Louis, Philippe and Jean Sénéclauze. Estate manager: Jean-Pierre Hugon. Vineyard manager: Jean-Louis Lajoux. Cellar master: Alain Gouinaud. **Size of vineyard:** 35 hectares. **Average age of vines:** 25 years. **Varieties:** 45% cabernet-sauvignon, 35% merlot, 15% cabernet-franc, 5% petit-verdot. **Production:** 150,000 bottles CB. **Direct sales:** tel. 56 88 30 01. **Marketing:** through the trade; Sté des Vins Sénéclauze, 164 boulevard de Plombières, 13307 Marseille Cedex.

Between the seventeenth and eighteenth centuries, Margaux and its surrounding areas saw the blossoming of a wealth of coats of arms, escutcheons, shields and crests of all sorts. From equerry to duke, Margaux has known them all. Many labels recall the sojourn, often transitory, of opportunist lords, true topers. Lord de Peguichan was, to quote Rostand's "Cyrano", one of those "courageous young men, bold musketeers, swordsmen from Gascony, knowing no peers". Through his mother's family, he was also the Marquis of Thermes, probably from Thermes d'Armagnac where good breeding shows. He courted one of the Ledoulx daughters,

153

de Rauzan's own niece, and led her to the altar on December 16, 1762. It is interesting that this date should be known with such precision for it is in fact the only one to be on record. The end of the eighteenth century has left no trace of this Gascon from the Médoc. Different authors relate that the vineyard comes about from the combination of several small *crus* spread over Cantenac, Margaux, Arsac and Soussans, whose names are today forgotten: Léoville-Cantenac, L'Isle, Sibille and Phénix. To date, I have not been able to retrace its real origins. It is also said that the *cru* of the Marquis de Thermes was formerly called MacDaniel. What is certain is that in the middle of the nineteenth century, a rich merchant called Oscar Sollberg gave back to the *cru* the fame it had lost. About the years 1830–40, he completely rebuilt the vineyard and it is thanks to this that it was classified as 4th *cru classé* in 1855. At that time, Sollberg was one of the most heavily taxed citizens in the commune of Margaux. He had epic struggles with the municipality concerning lands on the *palus* which he claimed to own. In point of fact Château Marquis de Termes does have vines on this loamy soil along the meadows by Château Margaux. For a long time before the creation of the Margaux AOC, a certain confusion existed between the wines which came from the gravelly soil and those from the loamy soil of the Marquis de Terme. The latter are today quite distinct and are sold under the name of "Château des Gondats". As far as the principal label is concerned, we note that the old spelling of Thermes has been simplified to Terme.

In his *Wine Encyclopaedia*, Alexis Lichine observes that the cultivation of the vineyards of the Marquis de Terme is impeccable but that the vinification is sometimes not up to standard. Anybody can verify the first part of this remark. All you have to do is to stroll round the village of Margaux where there are several parcels of vines growing alongside the houses. As for the second, it seems that the quality of the Marquis de Terme was not always what it should have been. But Château Marquis de Terme (which, moreover, has never had its own château as such) was notoriously under-equipped in the cellars, vat-house and other working buildings. Over the last few years, the present proprietors, the Sénéclauze family, have made a tremendous effort and brought about considerable improvements. The new cellars are huge, modern and well designed. A reception room welcomes visitors. The vat-house and the out-buildings are worthy of a *cru classé*.

The wine of the Marquis de Terme can be distinguished by its vigour and its robust character. Generally with a high tannin content, it is not always easy to drink in the first few years. Formerly, an excessively high proportion of petit-verdot underlined the fixed acidity. Today, I find the balance better, and curiously enough, it is in the off-years that the Marquis de Terme succeeds best by comparison with its neighbours. None the less, it always has a flavour of the land which, without ever achieving the great delicacy or extreme finesse of certain other wines of Margaux, reminds us that its former lord and master, Lord Peguichan, was a Gascon, pure and dour. The Marquis de Terme is on the way up.

Marsac Séguineau (Château)

cru bourgeois

Commune: Soussans. **Proprietor:** SC du Château Marsac Séguineau. Tel. 56 88 30 41. Manager: Patrice Baudieras, assisted by the oenologist Bernard Monteau. **Size of vineyard:** 8 hectares. **Average age of vines:** 17 years. **Varieties:** 2/3 cabernet-sauvignon, 1/3 merlot. **Production:** 35,000 bottles CB. **Marketing:** exclusively through Mestrezat SA, 17 cours de la Martinique, BP 90, 33027 Bordeaux Cedex. Tel. 56 52 11 46.

The coronet featured on this elegant, classically sober label is that of Count de Robieu who, in 1886, combined the *cru bourgeois* of Séguineau-Deyries with other parcels of vines in the area of Marsac. He did not give his name to the *cru*, for he considered that Marsac Séguineau had a better ring to it. At the beginning of the century, we find this *cru* in the possession of Madame Vast who increased the size of vineyard by buying several neighbouring parcels (probably coming from Lascombes or Malescot). Then the *cru* passed successively through the hands of the Marcelins, the Villefrancas and the Pécresses. The latter sold all their vineyards in Soussans, Avenasan, Moulis and Listrac to a firm of combined *grands crus* run by Lucien Lurton and the business firm of Mestrezat-Preller in Bordeaux (today, Mestrezat SA). But they divided their interests and split up with the result that Marsac Séguineau is under the control of Mestrezat.

This *cru* has two vineyards. They are both situated on the excellent terrain of Marsac. The soil is rather heavy, made up of clayey gravel. The wine is vinified in a rather modern way which diminishes its tannins but makes it slightly more supple. An advertising pamphlet recommends that it should be drunk between 14° and 16°C (i.e. 57°-61° F). Although personally I am not in favour of wines which are too warm, I think that a range of between 18°-20° C (64°-68° F) would be better, as for all the wines of Margaux.

Martinens (Château)

cru bourgeois supérieur

Commune: Cantenac. **Proprietor:** Simone Dulos and Jean-Pierre Seynat-Dulos. Manager: Jean-Pierre Seynat-Dulos (manager of the Société Fermière) and Madame Dulos (manager of the Société Civile). Estate manager: M. Delille. Cellar masters: M Delille and his son. **Size of vineyard:** 30 hectares. **Average age of vines:** 30 and 13 years. **Varieties:** 30% cabernet-sauvignon, 20% petit-verdot, 40% merlot, 10% cabernet-franc. **Production:** 85,000 bottles CB. **Direct sales and by mail order:** Château Martinens, Cantenac, 33460 Margaux. Tel. 56 88 71 37. **Marketing:** through the trade.

Situated on the extreme west of the commune of Cantenac and at the south-west of Margaux, Château Martinens's elegant residence is at the end of a little park surrounded by elegant railings which you enter by a wrought-iron gateway. The adjoining cellars and vat-house have a decided architectural congruity and are functional without being in any way tawdry. Everything is of correct dimensions – spacious without being too vast, sober but not austere, distinguished but not showy. There is always an exquisitely affable welcome at Martinens. I think this is sufficiently important to stress it. Madame Simone Dulos and her son, Jean-Pierre Seynat-Dulos, practise hospitality as some would yoga, with an inner warmth and conviction. This is contagious, for if the proprietors are absent, Monsieur Delille and his son will do everything to make the visitor feel at home as soon as he has first set foot in the cellar containing the latest vintage.

There is always the warmest of welcomes at Martinens.

In the eighteenth century, Ann, Jane and Mary White (who, being English, re-
sembled in some way the Brontë sisters) lived out one and the same novel, a story of
being in love with Martinens, which they owned jointly and which was a charming
second home for these three London women. In 1776, British affections were es-
tranged and the owner of the estate changed into Pierre Changeur, a wine-merchant
in Bordeaux. He extended its size and began the construction of the present château,
but sold up before completing all the modernizations he had envisaged. His suc-
156 cessor, Louis Mascou, who lived in Guadeloupe, also sold out, finding a buyer in

the person of the Count de Beauregard, alias François-Auguste de Sautter, Consul General of Tuscany and Chamberlain of the French Empire, who by this purchase hoped to be able to bring variety to the monotony of his white wines from the Swiss Canton of Vaud, produced on the family property of Beauregard. His daughters had the attractive names of Clémentine and Gertrude. When the Count de Beauregard died, they sold Martinens to Jules Jadouin, who was to be found more or less everywhere around Margaux at the end of the nineteenth century (*see* Angludet). His son-in-law, Louis-Jules Lebègue, directed it until 1936, as well as the commune Cantenac of which he was the leading magistrate. For nine years, Martinens fell again into Swiss hands before being owned by the Dulos-Seynat family. Jean-Pierre Seynat, who originally comes from the Landes, is the mayor of Cantenac. Is it because of the colourful history of Martinens that he is painted as a "gentleman-farmer"? His easygoing manner nicely hides his efficiency at making very good wine... and at leaving it to others to perceive this for themselves.

Maucaillou (Domaine de)

Commune: Soussans. **Proprietor:** Georges Rabi. Tel. 56 88 36 89. Manager: Marie Rabi. **Size of vineyard:** 2.5 hectares. **Average age of vines:** 20 to 25 years. **Varieties:** 30% cabernet, 60% merlot, 10% petit-verdot. **Production:** 12 tonneaux. **Marketing:** in bulk to the trade.

Maucaillou is a little locality of Soussans, a fairly common name in the Médoc, which means "poor pebbles". The plateau of Maucaillou is situated on the extreme northwest of the Margaux appellation in the region of Château Paveil. Apart from being made up of good soil of gravel and sandy gravel, this vineyard has one remarkable feature about it, namely that it covers exactly eight Bordeaux "journals". The size of vineyard of a "journal" (also called a "journau" or "journée") was the equivalent to the area of land a vigneron could work in one day. But

depending on the type of soil in the different viticultural regions and the nature of the slope, the dimension of the "journal" could change. The average for the gravelly soils was about 0.79 acres. The proprietors who employed a vigneron had a contract system called the "prix-fait" (agreed price). Each area of vines was subject to a contract, generally made up of eight "journals", that is to say about 2.55 hectares. A living witness to a past which mechanization has buried, Georges Rabi is his own "prix-faiteur" or contractor, and employs himself to cultivate his eight journals of cabernet, merlot and verdot. He should try to equip himself to be able to bottle his wine at the château.

At the age of 92, Madame Rabi's father was still in the vineyard.

Monbrison (Château)

cru bourgeois

Commune: Arsac. **Proprietor:** Elizabeth Davis and her sons. Director: Madame E. Davis assisted by her son Jean-Luc Vonderheyden. **Size of vineyard:** 15 hectares. **Average age of vines:** 24 years. **Varieties:** 30% merlot, 50% cabernet-sauvignon, 15% cabernet-franc, 5% petit-verdot. **Production:** 65,000 bottles CB. **Direct sales and by mail order:** in France. Château Monbrison, Arsac, 33460 Margaux. Tel. 56 88 82 21. **Marketing:** through the trade; sold directly to foreign importers.

Legend has it that an underground tunnel once linked Château d'Arsac to Monbrison and then carried onto the banks of the Gironde. So in case of attack, the besieged could flee. At the time, Monbrison was simply a huge meadow with a small house for the *métayer*. It has its origins in the early Middle Ages. The Conquéré de Monbrison family became its owners at the time of the Renaissance and retained it for more than a century. As the result of a joint family trust, half the land was detached from Château Desmirail, one of Margaux's third *grands crus classés*. In 1921, Robert Meacham-Davis, an American pastor, writer and journalist for the *Herald Tribune,* fell in love with Monbrison and Kathleen Johnston, the daughter of the famous Chartrons wine merchant Nathaniel Johnston, former Deputy for the Médoc and owner of Ducru-Beaucaillou, Dauzac, Château Trompette and, last of all, Château Cordet which today has reappeared as Monbrison's second label.

The estate of Monbrison assumed its present outline during the 1960s. There are 25 hectares of gravelly land whose vineyard accounts for 15 hectares in one unbroken stretch. The château is a charming, romantic manor-house standing on the plateau and surrounded by a parkland of unusual pines.

Robert and Kathleen's daughter, Elizabeth M. Davis (Betty, to her friends) and her three sons, Bruno, Jean-Luc and Laurent Vonderheyden are devoted to this appealing terrain. The vines and vinification are their one love.

A refined intimate atmosphere contributes to the charm of Monbrison.

The wine of Monbrison is robust, deep with a touch of tenderness, tannic and generous. It deserves to be laid down for a while. After ageing, it has a harmonious, well-balanced bouquet. Tribute should be paid to the progress made since the beginning of the 1980s. The Vonderheyden brothers are by now well known for their ardent quest of quality. Their outspokenness sometimes irritates their environment but Monbrison has undoubtedly raised itself to the top of the list of the *crus bourgeois* in the Margaux appellation. So has its price!

Moncabon (Enclos de) ♟→ *Rauzan-Gassies*

Mongravey (Château)

Commune: Arsac. **Proprietor:** Régis Bernaleau. **Size of vineyard:** 4.30 hectares. **Average age of vines:** 18 years for 1.80 hectares, the rest, very old. **Varieties:** 54% cabernet-sauvignon, 37% merlot, 9% cabernet-franc. **Production:** 15,000 bottles CB. **Direct sales and by mail order:** Château Mongravey, Arsac, 33460 Margaux. Tel. 56 58 84 51. **Marketing:** through the trade.

Château Mongravey is a recent creation resulting from the combination of a few parcels of land in the commune of Arsac. Régis Bernaleau succeeds his father and has carefully preserved the foundation of the vineyard – grape varieties whose years are beyond being counted. A small half has been replanted over the last eighteen years. Within three or four years he hopes to be able to produce about 25,000 bottles and he is now looking to sell direct, although he continues to supply the Bordeaux wine-trade.

Not very far from Château Monbrison, Mongravey also endeavours to read its neighbour's level of quality.

Montbrun (Château)

cru bourgeois

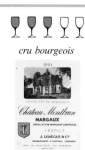

Commune: Cantenac. **Proprietor:** J. Lebègue & Cie SA. Managers: Jacques and Alain de Coninck. Vineyard manager: M. Munes. **Size of vineyard:** 8 hectares. **Average age of vines:** 20 years. **Varieties:** 75% merlot, 25% cabernet. **Production:** 40,000 bottles CB. **Marketing:** J. Lebègue et Cie SA, 33330 Saint-Emilion. Tel. 57 51 31 05.

At the time when the Péreires bought Palmer, they were not able to restore it to what it had been when the famous general had originally created it. There were different pieces missing in the jigsaw puzzle, scattered about by the former proprietor because of his financial difficulties. At that time the Jadouin family owned a large area of vines situated principally in Cantenac. It was Jules Jadouin who created the *cru* of Monbrun (without a "t") based on an area featuring on the Land Register by this name which had been cut off from Palmer. Then at the very end of the last century, his son-in-law Jacques Lebègue had a large mansion built, designed by Monsieur Minvielle, "one of the most distinguished architects of Bordeaux". Château Montbrun was named a *cru bourgeois supérieur*. (It is amusing to note that the most recent editions of Féret's *Bordeaux et ses vins* continue to praise the architecture of the château, although it was completely destroyed by fire in 1956.) In the middle of the hamlet of Issan, of which, after Palmer, it occupies the larger part, Montbrun long served as a storage cellar for the firm of J. Lebègue & Co. The present partners, Jacques and Alain de Coninck, now use a storage cellar in Saint-Emilion, so Montbrun's working buildings have been restored to their original use.

The terrain of Montbrun now consists of several parcels of which the heart is, of course, the former area of Palmer. Merlot predominates, which is very rare in the Margaux appellation. Montbrun produces supple, rich and unctuous wines which suit the clients in the north of France and Europe where they are widely distributed and appreciated. Equivalent to Pontac-Lynch and Vincent, situated in the same part of Issan, in the commune of Cantenac, Château Montbrun is a typical Margaux *cru bourgeois*.

Moulin de Tricot (Château)

Commune: Arsac. **Proprietor:** Claude Rey. Consultant oenologist: M. Couasnon. **Size of vineyard:** 1.67 hectares. **Varieties:** 75% cabernet-sauvignon, 25% merlot. **Production:** 8,000 bottles, the rest to the trade. **Visits:** Tel. 56 58 83 55. **Direct sales and by mail order:** in France: Claude Rey, Arsac, 33460 Margaux.

For pleasure and out of deep family loyalty, Claude Rey took on the old vineyard of his in-laws, the Gravier-Lalandes. After ten years of being untended (since 1972) for reasons of health, the little vineyard formerly run by Albert Lalande has been taken in hand once more and intelligently replanted. On this land, the intelligent thing to have done is to have given pre-eminence to the cabernet-sauvignon which flourishes happily here. When all the wine is bottled, Moulin de Tricot (an old name which makes one think of granny and her knitting) will be able to hold its head high among the wines of Margaux.

Notton-Baury (Château) 🍾→ Brane-Cantenac

Palmer (Château)

3e cru classé

Commune: Cantenac. **Proprietor:** SCI Château Palmer. Manager: B. Bouteiller. Vineyard manager: Claude Chardon. Cellar master: Yves Chardon. **Size of vineyard:** 45 hectares. **Average age of vines:** 35 years. **Varieties:** 55% cabernet-sauvignon, 39% merlot, 6% cabernet-franc. **Production:** 150,000 bottles CB. **Marketing:** exclusively through the trade; Sté Sichel, 19 quai de Bacalan, 33000 Bordeaux; Sté Mähler-Besse, 49 rue Camille-Godard, 33000 Bordeaux.

Ten years ago, Professor Pijassou, a pupil of Henri Enjalbert and a tireless chronicler of the vineyards of the Médoc, wrote a lengthy article on Château Palmer in *La Revue historique de Bordeaux et du département de la Gironde.* On reading this impressive and erudite text, we learn much about the condition of the vignerons of the eighteenth century, about the great families of the Médoc, about the viticultural Land Register of the commune of Cantenac towards the end of the *ancien régime,* and about the House of Foix de Candale, the barony of Issan and the seigniory of Angludet. Pierre d'Aulède, the proprietor of Margaux and Haut-Brion is often quoted, as are the famous priests Baurein and Bellet. It is interesting to note that this text confirms that there was considerable business carried out by river, which in my opinion has been tremendously underestimated in the history of the development of the vineyards of the Médoc. But the history of Château Palmer, prior to the nineteenth century, has only lightly been touched on. I would certainly not have the pretension to go further back in time than René Pijassou or to try to do better. So I will leave him to comment: "It would seem that another portion of the estate of Issan had passed into the Gasq family, of which several members belonged to the Parlement de Bordeaux. At the end of the eighteenth century, Madame Marie Burnet de La Ferrière, the widow of Monsieur Blaise-Jean-Charles-Alexandre de Gasq, was the sole proprietor. This was essentially a vineyard of some 50 hectares in Cantenac and Margaux. It produced a great wine, known at Versailles as Château de Gasq." Here, Professor Pijassou cites as his reference the *Statistique générale de la Gironde* by Edouard Féret in his 1874 edition. As far as I know, nothing has ever proved this assertion. As for Versailles... and Richelieu who was extremely fond of the *cru* of de Gasq, this probably belongs to local traditional legend. None the less, Monsieur Pijassou was quite right in thinking that Issan was already divided up half a century before the Revolution. This considerable estate was predestined to be split up and divided out among such a large family over the generations. Traces of the de Gasqs can be found in the social, economic and political life of Bordeaux and, most probably, fashion more or less obliged them to take an active interest in the vineyards of the Médoc in the same way that managing directors from Paris have a hunt in Sologne to the south of the Loire. (The de Gasq – or Gasques – family probably originated from the present-day department of Tarn-et-Garonne.) What is more, once a vineyard is detached from its original estate, it becomes an anonymous orphan. Everything leads us to believe that Gasq gave his name to the lands separated from Issan, formerly Théobon. Moreover, did not the jury of 1855 rightly confirm the previous situation by classifying the two neighbours Issan and Palmer as 3e *crus*?

When Gasq died, his widow managed to survive the Reign of Terror, though with difficulty, but she was unable to pay the death duties. In 1814, she sold Château de Gasq (the sale contract refers to "the estate of Issan") to Major-General Charles Palmer, an officer on the general staff of the Prince of Wales and one of Wellington's staff officers. Why did he come to Bordeaux? He probably stopped off on his way

Hosts of tourists stop in front of Palmer's neo-Renaissance façade.

back from the campaign in Spain after the defeat of Napoleon at Vittoria. The surrender of Paris was signed on April 11, 1814, and the purchase of Issan on June 16. From that moment, he was a different man. Over twenty years, Palmer extended his land on all sides. He bought up whatever he could, beginning with a considerable part of Dubignon-Talbot (*see* Larruau). Seized with an insatiable hunger for vines, he made acquisition after acquisition, the most notable being a part of Montbrun, the heathlands of Boston and other land in Issan. But in 1834, his wife decided to cut the matrimonial purse-strings and mortgage the estate. As from that moment there was a slow but inexorable collapse. The mortgage loan office took possession of Château Palmer in 1844 and administered it for the following

ten years until its acquisition by the Péreires. A family of Portuguese Jews, the Péreires had the talent for spotting the best property investments. (They also had great ability: Arcachon was of their creation.)

Isaac Rodrigue-Péreire, the great rival of the Rothschilds, bought Palmer just before the 1855 classification. It was too late to influence the course of events and to raise the *cru* to a higher level. But this great family did not take long in restoring the vineyard which had been ravaged by mildew and in building a château on yet one more piece of land taken from Issan. It is often said that Palmer is above its classification. Here, I venture to suggest that *if Palmer, Issan and the other lands of the ancient Houses of Foix de Candale and Castelnau d'Essenault had been* 163 *integrally preserved, they would jointly have been a* premier cru classé. It should not be forgotten that in the Médoc, quality comes from the size and the variety of the terrains... provided they are the best. In 1938, Palmer was split up. A financial company was formed, which is still the owner of the *cru*. Its shareholders are the Mählers and the Sichels.

It is fitting here to make special mention of the "three Chardons": the father, Pierre and the two sons Claude and Yves (plus the grandsons), who are true servants of duty and are the real creators of this *chef d'œuvre*. The wines of Palmer can be outstandingly successful. There is a balance between body and finesse comparable with the harmony of Greek architecture. But I will leave an Englishman the last word – Nicholas Faith writing about Château Margaux: "Its next-door neighbour on the south side, Château Palmer, whose sunny slopes are next to those of Margaux's best land, is the only one in the commune which, in certain years, can be compared to it." Thank you both, Pijassou and Faith: I think you are both right.

Paveil de Luze (Château)

cru bourgeois

Commune: Soussans. **Proprietor:** GFA du Château Paveil. Tel. 56 88 30 03. **Manager:** Geoffroy de Luze, assisted by René Fort. **Size of vineyard:** 24 hectares. **Average age of vines:** 15 years. **Varieties:** 70% cabernet-sauvignon, 30% merlot. **Production:** 120,000 bottles CB. **Marketing:** through the trade; Groupement Français des Vins (GFV) in Bordeaux.

With its 15 hectares of park, moorland and gardens, its seventeenth century château-cum-cellars and its 24 hectares of vines spread out like a fan in front of the wrought iron gateway like a green carpet with white pebbles dotted about on it, Paveil is the estate of your dreams. You would think it had come straight out of a child's picture book with here, the part of the house which is lived in, and there, the cellars, vat-house and the farm, and further away, the little corner where the workers have their living quarters, and further on, between the château and the forest, the lake (fed by a spring of clear water which supplies all the estate) in which you can fish tench, carp and pike. And at harvest-time, you can get up early to go for a walk in the forest and gather *cèpe* and *chanterelle* mushrooms. The Luzes have been at Paveil for more than a century. At the beginning of the nineteenth century, an aristocratic family from Neuchâtel emigrated to the United States. Young Alfred and Louis-Philippe, who were then adolescents, related this adventure with enthusiasm. They became importers of rare and expensive foodstuffs, including wine. After a while, Alfred came back to Europe looking for worthwhile suppliers and a port for shipping the goods. Bordeaux fulfilled his requirements. He settled there and bought Paveil in 1862 from a wine merchant from Saint-Domingue, M. Minvielle. The estate had been created during the reign of Louis XIII by the Chevalier de Bretonneau on lands which his wife (yet one more daughter of the Rauzan family) brought him as a dowry. The distinguishing feature of these buildings is that they are all under one roof, both the living quarters and the working buildings. The weekend guest at Paveil can get up during the night, if he is thirsty, and drink a sample of the new wine without having to step out of doors.

The wine of Paveil is as distinguished as its proprietor. It tends to be more delicate than sturdy. The bitterness of its early youth quickly changes into bouquet. It ages well, preserving its charm and suppleness. The vineyards are planted on three plateaux of very dense, deep gravel. It is one of the best filtering soils in the

At Paveil, a single roof shelters the owner and the wines he makes.

Margaux appellation, which is why the yields per hectare are among the smallest. The proprietors of Château Paveil de Luze have created a Groupement Foncier Agricole, consisting of Baron Geoffroy de Luze and his three children, Madame Denis Blanchard-Dignac, Monsieur Frédéric de Luze and Mademoiselle Catherine de Luze. An advance sentry on the extreme northwest tip of the Margaux appellation, Paveil de Luze has faithfully stood guard for nearly four centuries now.

Pavillon Blanc du Château Margaux

Commune: Soussans. **Proprietor:** SCA Château Margaux. 33460 Margaux. **Size of vineyard:** 11 hectares. **Varieties:** 100% sauvignon blanc. **Production:** 40,000 bottles CB. **Marketing:** through the trade.

Formerly reserved for the proprietor's personal consumption and produced in undeclared quantities, the Pavillon Blanc du Château Margaux has increased its production both in quantity and quality over the last generation. Its sale price too has increased.

Pavillon Rouge
du Château Margaux 🍷→ Margaux

Pichecan (Château de)

Commune: Soussans. **Proprietor:** Jean-Marc Boutain. **Size of vineyard:** 3.5 hectares. **Average age of vines:** 18 years. **Varieties:** 60% cabernet-sauvignon, 30% merlot, 10% petit-verdot. **Production:** 15,000 bottles CB. **Direct sales and by mail order:** in France and abroad. Château de Pichecan, Le Grand-Soussans, 33460 Margaux. Tel. 56 88 73 04 or 56 88 77 09 (evenings).

In Féret's earlier editions of *Bordeaux et ses vins*, as from 1886, mention is made of a *cru bourgeois* by the name of Château Grand-Soussans. Today, this name has disappeared, having produced very irregularly. Jean-Marc Boutain lives in Le Grand-Soussans which is a small part of the commune. His little empire of 5.50 hectares, of which more than half is under vines, makes up the kingdom of Pichecan, a name you would say had been taken from a mediaeval novel, but whose real meaning in local dialect is less than poetic.

Having said this, I should warn you that to be able to drink a pitcher of Pichecan, you will have to get up early and to be in favour with Jean-Marc Boutain. For the Lord Chief Justice of Pichecan is very choosy about whom he selects as customers for his wine.

Pontac-Lynch (Château)

cru bourgeois supérieur

Commune: Margaux. **Proprietor:** GFA du Château Pontac-Lynch. Manager: Madame Bondon. **Size of vineyard:** 9 hectares. **Average age of vines:** 20 years. **Varieties:** 45% cabernet, 50% merlot, 5% petit-verdot. **Production:** 35,000 to 40,000 bottles CB. **Direct sales and by mail order:** in France and abroad. Château Pontac-Lynch, 33460 Margaux. Tel. 56 88 30 04.

How extraordinary the association of these two names is! They combine our conception of two top-class names, representing the quintessence of great wines in the eighteenth and nineteenth centuries. Over an area of five to seven hundred yards, as the crow flies, you can see a semicircle of *crus* round Château Margaux. In a clockwise direction, we have Issan, Montbrun, Vincent, Palmer, Rausan-Ségla, Rauzan-Gassies (and the Marquis de Terme slightly off course), Durfort-Vivens, Malescot Saint-Exupéry, Larruau, Desmirail-Marquis d'Alesme Becker and La Gurgue. Here I am mentioning only the châteaux as such, not necessarily the vineyards which are sometimes spread about all over the appellation. But what has become of Pontac-Lynch? If you are not looking at the hours and minutes on this clock face, you must look at the seconds. Indeed, Pontac-Lynch is the second finger in the middle of this neatly arranged dial. It is hidden at the end of a drive of palm trees which an early-twentieth-century Tartarin brought back from his conquest in Algeria. It is very small, I agree, but it is there, straddling the boundary of the gravelly soil and the loamy soils, like its neighbours Château Issan on the left and Château Margaux on the right. You would say that it was one of Sempé's drawings depicting a little French café, with three bicycles in front of the door, squashed in between two

The late Serge Bondon on the palm-bordered road leading to Pontac-Lynch.

distinguished palaces in front of which the latest models of limousines are parked. It is Pontac-Lynch! Such a distinguished neighbourhood has given the *cru* several complexes. Firstly, it is small in size (ten times smaller than Château Margaux); secondly, its vines are rather low (maybe, but the drainage is perfect, and moreover, several areas of heavy soil give the plants a certain vigour). Between 1741 and 1774, as the eminent Professor Pijassou has mentioned, Pontac-Lynch used to sell its production at a higher price than the very great *crus* which were later placed in a position of honour in the 1855 classification. Serge Bondon, who died recently in the prime of life, was aiming to restore Pontac-Lynch to a position of wide renown. We hope that his successors will strain every nerve to do just that.

Pontet-Chappaz (Château)

Commune: Arsac. **Proprietor:** SA Vignobles Rocher Cap-de-Rive, 33350 Saint-Magne de Castillon. Tel. 57 40 08 88. Director: Jean Lafaye. Consultant oenologist: Michel Rolland. Tel. 57 40 18 28. Estate manager: M. Caussan in Ordonnac. **Size of vineyard:** 7 hectares. **Average age of vines:** 16 years. **Varieties:** 60% cabernet-sauvignon, 30% merlot, 10% cabernet-franc. **Production:** 40,000 bottles CB. **Marketing:** SNC Pontet Ferrand, 33350 Saint-Magne de Castillon.

Monsieur Geens lives in Belgium, where he runs, from afar, several vineyards in the department of Gironde of which Château Pontet-Chappaz in Arsac is one. This vineyard of seven hectares in one unbroken stretch is planted on a fine terrace of gravelly soil by the side of Monbrison. Since 1986, this château has had a vat- 167 house for up-to-date vinification and a cellar for ageing which were both badly needed. Formerly, the harvest used to be transported to Saint-Germain d'Esteuil, near Lesparre. I think that Pontet-Chappaz is now running on the rails of progress. A label to be followed closely.

Portet, Nadine

Commune: Soussans. **Proprietor:** Nadine Portet, Tayac, Soussans, 33460 Margaux. Tel. 56 88 33 06. **Size of vineyard:** 0.57 hectares. **Average age of vines:** 20 years. **Varieties:** 65% cabernet-sauvignon, 35% merlot. **Production:** 35 hectolitres for 1986. **Marketing:** through the trade; Ets Salin in Bordeaux. *One of the smallest vineyards in the Margaux AOC which will one day, I hope, do its own bottling. It should increase to 1.5 hectares for the 1990 harvest.*

Pouget (Château)

4e cru classé

Commune: Cantenac. **Proprietor:** GFA des Châteaux Boyd-Cantenac et Pouget. Manager and director: Pierre Guillemet. Consultant oenologist: M. Emile Peynaud. **Size of vineyard:** 10 hectares. **Average age of vines:** 25 years. **Varieties:** 66% cabernet-sauvignon, 30% merlot, 4% cabernet-franc. **Production:** 47,000 bottles CB. **Direct sales and by mail order:** in France. Château Pouget, Cantenac, 33460 Margaux. Tel. 56 88 30 58. **Marketing:** through the trade; Messrs. Dubos Frères et Cie, 24 quai des Chartrons, 33000 Bordeaux.

At first this was the wine of the canon of Saint-Emilion, the chaplain of La Majorale in Bordeaux, a man of substantial income and robust constitution which led him towards wines of quality, much to the advantage of his flock, dazzled by his talented eloquence. He was called Etienne Monteil and carried out his ministry during the second part of the seventeenth century.

One hundred years later, the sacerdotal land came into the hands of François-Antoine Pouget, the residuary legatee of a branch of the Monteil-Dorchiac-Ducasse families. He did not refuse this heaven-sent gift and gave it his name, very honourably known as that of a well-to-do man of Bordeaux who was elected to many public offices. Claire, his beautiful but only daughter, married the man she well deserved – Pierre-François de Chavaille, a young and brilliant lawyer, and secretary-general to the City of Bordeaux.

In the nineteenth century, Pouget, like many other *crus,* underwent changes on the Land Register as a result of sales and splitting up through inheritances. It was often rated with the third *crus* before the 1855 classification. But that took place at a time when Château Pouget was not in the peak of condition and it was classed among the fourths. In 1906, the Elie-Guillemet family became the proprietors. Monsieur P. Elie managed to buy two hectares at Rauzan-Gassies on the south slope of the vineyard in Cantenac. Pierre Guillemet, who also owns Château Boyd-Cantenac, is an excellent viticulturalist. As to vinification, he is helped by Professor Emile Peynaud.

The arms of the Chavaille family still feature on the label. Formerly, they were followed by a nicely turned epigram which described the heraldic positions: gules, heart argent; azure, cock argent; sable, lion rampant or. I cannot resist the lyricism of the last verse: "Fond love o'er your heart its sure force will extend, / Your speech shall ring clear as the crow of the cock, / And like to the lion you will ne'er feel the shock / By drinking this wine which doth others transcend." In my opinion, there are two more lines needed today to complete the poem: "Its elegance, perfume and charm of a friend / Make Château Pouget a delicious Médoc."

Prieuré-Lichine (Château)

4e cru classé

Commune: Cantenac. **Proprietor:** SA Château Prieuré Lichine. Vineyard manager: Albert Birades. Cellar master: Armand Labarère. **Size of vineyard:** 61 hectares. **Varieties:** 55% cabernet-sauvignon, 31% merlot, 7% petit-verdot, 7% cabernet-franc. **Production:** 230,000 bottles CB. **Direct sales and by mail order:** Château Prieuré-Lichine, Cantenac, 33460 Margaux. Tel. 56 88 36 28. **Marketing:** through the trade; all the big firms in Bordeaux.

Prieuré is in deep mourning. Its lord and master is no more, and with him disappears one of the figures predominant in the Bordeaux wine world since the Second World War. A citizen of the United States of America of Russian origin, he had well and truly found his *raison d'être* and new cultural roots in the Médoc. I have had innumerable contacts with him and we were neighbours for close on forty years. I salute the memory of this endearing and forceful personality. I could not count the number of occasions we have drunk wines together, but several times, I have been witness to his abilities as a taster and to his expert judgement. He was an aesthetic, an epicurean, who loved good things and who was a man of exemplary good taste. Alexis Lichine was an institution in himself. I called him "the Father Prior", which used to make him burst into fits of laughter.

Château Prieuré-Lichine has no clear written trace of former monks, but this last one did not succeed through backstairs influence, for he stepped boldly into the story through the main door of the vat-house. His saintly, canonical virtues, his devout hospitality, his Benedictine erudition in the matter of wine and the extent and success of his evangelical mission throughout the world earned him the sobriquet of "High Pontiff of Wine" from a New York journalist to whom he had once made his confession. When Alexis Lichine bought Prieuré, a 4th *cru classé*, in 1951, all that remained were 11 hectares of ailing vines, cellars overrun with bats and a dark, draughty, derelict dwelling. What he has done with all this is remarkable, controversial and admirable.

Remarkable, because within thirty-five years he has given back to the *cru* the fame which it had long since lost. The vineyard was started again from scratch. At first, several exchanges with neighbours, notably Emmanuel Cruse who was trying to reorganize the land at Issan. Then acquisitions, parcel by parcel, sometimes even just two or three rows. And he also leased a lot of land in the best possible areas. The cellars were renovated in stages, as were the vat-houses and the other working buildings. During this time, Father Alexis created a comfortable manor-house and managed to give it the authentic appearance of a château. He brought along all his finds from the antique shops in the southwest as well as several paintings by contemporary masters, including the finest Fontanarosa I have ever seen. In order that foreign photographers who came to shoot him could give the story complete

The late Alexis Lichine at Prieuré in his priory garden.

coverage, he has a huge Pyrenean sheep-dog and a collie answering to the names of Bacchus and Margaux. Speaking of dogs, I think it amusing to record here what the famous humorist Art Buchwald wrote in Prieuré's visitors' book: "1959 was a great year for the wines of Bordeaux. And for me too visiting this region. From now on, I shall not be able to look at a bunch of grapes without seeing him (Lichine) and his big dogs, so fond of the parish priest's chickens. In this context, an agreement has been reached whereby the priest is to receive one bottle of wine for every chicken killed by his dogs and he will celebrate a special Requiem Mass for each dog killed by one of the chickens."

Controversial because right at the outset, Alexis Lichine's publicity methods were at variance with the traditional restraint of the Bordeaux, Chartrons and Médoc "establishment". With an innate sense of theatre and a pronounced taste for staging, he has played in a hundred-act comedy, – a comedy which he wrote as he was filling his salon and dining-room. For the majority of foreign journalists coming to Bordeaux, a visit to Alexis and his Prieuré was a must. None the less, Lichine has truly created a new style of conviviality which we may or may not like though it is every bit as admirable as that of Philippe de Rothschild.

Admirable. The achievement of this exceptional man is admirable and if we were sometimes aggravated by the huge stature of the man (a single wave of his hand displaced 200 cubic feet of air), we must bow before his memory. He attracted an ocean of importers, distributors, restaurateurs and wine lovers who have spread all over the Bordeaux region. Indeed, he carefully channelled the major part (and he did well to do so), much to the prejudice of certain competitors who nevertheless enjoyed substantial leftovers. But from 1950 to 1980, Lichine made known far and wide (especially in the U.S.A.) the wines of France and those of Bordeaux, with a "zoom" effect focused on the Médoc and Margaux.

With its 61 hectares of vines planted all over the appellation, and its ultra-modern spacious cellars, Château Prieuré-Lichine is today a very great Margaux *cru* which has placed itself above its official rating as a fourth *cru*. The diversity of its land gives a richness of complementary qualities enhanced by the different varieties of grapes. Doubtless, certain parcels of vines are not quite old enough. But viewed overall and entirely objectively, the wine produced by Château Prieuré-Lichine attains a level of quality which from one vintage to the next makes it competitive with all the wines of Margaux. It is now up to Sacha, Alexis's son, to continue his father's work. He is capable of doing so, as he showed in 1989, when he did not hesitate to start harvesting weeks earlier than some of his neighbours. Physically, as well as viticulturally, Sacha seems to have slipped comfortably into his father's shoes, an excellent augury for the future of the estate.

Pys (Domaine du)

Commune: Arsac. **Proprietor:** Gilbert Sallebert. **Size of vineyard:** 0.7 hectares. **Average age of vines:** 15 years. **Varieties:** 54% cabernet-sauvignon, 30% merlot, 16% cabernet-franc. **Production:** between 28 and 30 hectolitres. **Direct sales:** essentially to friends and private customers. Gilbert Sallebert, Le Pys, Arsac, 33460 Margaux. Tel. 56 58 86 06. **Marketing:** through the trade. *This little vineyard has been officially recognized as a Margaux AOC since 1982. It is nearly impossible to buy any from the Bordeaux trade.*

Quatre Vents (Clos des)

Commune: Soussans. **Proprietor:** René Renaud. **Size of vineyard:** 3 hectares. **Average age of vines:** 20 years. **Varieties:** traditional. **Production:** 12,000 bottles CB. **Direct sales and by mail order:** in France. Clos des Quatre Vents, Bourriche, Soussans, 33460 Margaux. Tel. 56 88 30 87. **Marketing:** through the trade.

The Château of the "Four Winds" is one which has resisted well over the years – "come wind, come weather". René Renaud is the great-grandson of an old Soussans vigneron family. His little vineyard of 3 hectares is practically in the village itself and seems to serve as a sundial marked by the shadow of the village church spire. The other part is in Marsac, the best gravelly slope in Soussans, on the boundary of the commune of Margaux. René Renaud is an accomplished taster, which is a complementary quality of a good grower. It is one thing to cultivate vines, another to harvest and make wine, and yet another to look after and develop the wine up to the moment of bottling. To be able to choose the ideal moment for the various jobs on the vineyard or in the cellar is essential to success, and it is by tasting rather than by chemical analysis that the right time for racking is determined. The Clos des Quatre Vents and René Renaud together make a wine with a fine bouquet which surprises by its suppleness on the palate. What is also agreeably surprising is its sale price: one of the most reasonable in the Margaux AOC.

Rambaud (Château)

Commune: Soussans. **Proprietor:** André Fort. **Size of vineyard:** 1.48 hectares. **Average age of vines:** 50 years. **Varieties:** 40% cabernet-sauvignon, 50% merlot, 10% petit-verdot. **Production:** 5,000 bottles CB. **Direct sales:** to individual customers. Tel. 56 88 32 62.

A distinctly British influence can be seen in the style of the roofs at Rausan-Ségla.

Rausan-Ségla (Château)

2e cru classé

Commune: Margaux. **Proprietor:** Holt Frères et Fils. President: Jacques Théo. Director: René Baffert. Estate manager: Michel Bruzaud. **Size of vineyard:** 43 hectares. **Average age of vines:** 23 years. **Varieties:** 66% cabernet-sauvignon, 28% merlot, 4% cabernet-franc, 2% petit-verdot. **Production:** 168,000 to 192,000 bottles CB. **Direct sales and by mail order:** in France. Château Rausan-Ségla, 33460 Margaux. Tel. 56 88 70 30. **Marketing:** through the trade; Louis Eschenauer SA, 42 avenue Emile Counord, 33300 Bordeaux. Tel. 56 81 58 90.

For centuries, the wine of Rausan was at the head of the second *crus* of the Médoc. The 1855 classification honoured Rausan-Ségla and Rauzan-Gassies, citing them immediately after Mouton (the distinction of Rausan with an "s" and Rauzan with a "z" goes back to the end of the nineteenth century). The two *crus* became

Rausan in the time of Senator Durand-Dassié.

divided under the Revolution in troubled circumstances. If we consider this period in a strictly viticultural context, we find in Margaux alone a great deal of upheavals among the large estates. At the beginning of the sixteenth century, the noble House of Gassies was predominant. We find Gaillard de Tardes in 1530 and Bernard de Faverolles in 1615. Then in 1661, it seems that the wealthy merchant, Pierre des Mesures de Rausan, bought the estate at the same time as he was leasing Château Margaux and, a little later, Château Latour. Three good runners. As for Rausan and Rauzan, this is rather like the story of the Smiths and the Smythes. Different authors have different opinions without really contradicting one another about the exact history of the *cru*. It seems to be an established fact that at the end of the seventeenth century Pierre des Mesures de Rausan owned a large number of vineyards. But we find trace of the purchase of the land of Gassies (or Garcies) in 1775 by another Monsieur Rauzan who was a member of the Parlement de Bordeaux. In fact, for two centuries this estate was sometimes divided up and sometimes reunited. The last descendant of the Rausans, Baroness de Castelpers, sold Rausan-Ségla in 1866 to Senator Eugène Durand-Dassié who afterwards handed it onto his son-in-law, Frédéric Cruse. Monsieur de Meslon was owner for a short time between 1956 and 1960, at which date the Liverpool firm of maritime suppliers, John Holt, bought the estate before taking on the Bordeaux firm of wine merchants, Louis Eschenauer.

At the time of the 1855 classification, the two Rausans, as I said, were at the head of the second *crus* just after Mouton. This position established a certain reputation, reflecting the snobbishness of connoisseurs: "I do not buy Château Margaux because it is too expensive, but the neighbouring *cru* Rausan is better value." This reputation spread especially in England, where Monsieur de Rausan (or Rauzan?), adroit wine merchant that he was, knew how to organize his publicity. Towards the middle of the eighteenth century, impatient to sell his harvest, which he considered exceptional, he had it put on board a merchant ship and accompanied it in person to London. From his floating cellar, near the famous Tower of London, he sent samples of his *cru* to all the wine lovers of the London gentry. It was a great success story and word spread in the salons of Kensington and St. James. But the seller's asking price was such that there were fewer orders than spectators. When the latter were gathered in sufficient number, M. de Rausan ordered the sailors to throw a cask into the Thames, a vivid way of putting a message in a cask to say that the bids were not high enough. Just like the hawker who breaks his pile of plates on the pavement when he cannot find a buyer, he discharged a second cask into the river, then a third, each time raising the sale price of the wine which remained in proportion to the loss. When it came to the fourth cask, hands went up on the quayside by the Tower of London and the happy proprietor was able to realize his floating capital.

The wine of Rausan-Ségla is one of the finest in the Margaux appellation. Its poor terrain predisposes it to a certain thinness, but it expresses it with a rare elegance. On the other hand, it rarely succeeds in years of cold and rain. Then, as Tristan Bernard said, speaking of a very weak coffee: "Its virtues come close to frailty." You have to be a great lover of delicate wine with a fine bouquet, and music played pianissimo to appreciate Rausan-Ségla in all its discreet subtlety. It is a wine for dining by candlelight and whispers, accompanied by exquisite dishes and an intimate friend. If it has been said many times that the wines of Margaux are feminine, Rausan-Ségla is the very essence of this femininity.

Rauzan-Gassies (Château)

2e cru classé

Commune: Margaux. **Proprietor:** SCI de Château Rauzan-Gassies. Manager: Madame Paul Quié and J.-M. Quié. Vineyard manager: Marc Espagnet. Cellar master: Jean-Marc Espagnet. **Size of vineyard:** 30 hectares. **Average age of vines:** 25 to 30 years. **Varieties:** 40% cabernet-sauvignon, 39% merlot, 20% cabernet-franc, 1% petit-verdot. **Production:** 100,000 bottles CB. **Direct sales and by mail order:** Château Rauzan-Gassies, 33460 Margaux, tel. 56 88 71 88 or SCI Rauzan-Gassies, 135 rue de Paris, 94220 Charenton. Tel. (1) 43 68 08 41. **Marketing:** through the trade; several large firms in Bordeaux.

Rauzan-Gassies was separated from the great estate of Rauzan towards the end of the eighteenth century. This vineyard is a jigsaw puzzle whose scattered pieces are entirely representative of the principal types of terrain in Margaux. We find heavy gravel soil, sandy gravel with a clayey or ferruginous subsoil. Certain vines are in the very heart of the village of Margaux. The "château", which is in fact a collection of working buildings, is by the side of Château Rausan-Ségla. When you come from Bordeaux and reach the sign marking the entrance to the village of Margaux, you can see the two Rausans by the side of the park of Durfort directly on your left.

Paul Quié bought Rauzan-Gassies in 1943. Today, his wife and his son, Jean-Michel, run the vineyard with the help of Monsieur Espagnet and his son. After a short time during which its fame declined, this label has now caught up again with the second *crus* and it sells at more or less the same price as the wines of 175

Rausan-Ségla, Brane and Lascombes. Whereas the majority of the *grands crus* in the Margaux appellation have undergone extensive changes on the Land Register since 1855, Rauzan-Gassies has more or less stayed as it originally was. Mention must be made of the beneficial influence of the then proprietor, Monsieur Rhoné-Pereire, at the end of the nineteenth century. But its very great reputation goes back to the time of M. de Rauzan, a member of the Parlement de Bordeaux. It is said that within twenty years, he created a model estate out of this property, and that he had exceptional skill as a vintner. To such an extent that the local vignerons accused him of sorcery. The people of the village used to turn round after he had gone by and make the sign of the Cross, and the ploughmen who worked for him used to sew millet in their trouser turn-ups. One year, frost affected all the neighbouring vineyards except that of Rauzan. Suspicion began to grow. But the last straw was when a huge hailstorm curiously spared the vines of Rauzan just a few days before harvesting was due to begin. The pickers and porters making up his team of harvesters were panic stricken and would not start harvesting. Realizing the danger, he called together all the peasants of Margaux in his cellar and said: "You think that I am a sorcerer. That is completely untrue." An old man made bold: "And yet, Monsieur de Rauzan, we have been told that you are a Freemason." "Yes, I took up Freemasonry for its good points. There is nothing supernatural about that. On the contrary, everything is quite natural. I will reveal my secret." The peasants pricked up their ears, awaiting the revelation. "You claim that I have made a pact with the Devil and that demons come nightly to work on my vines. You say that you have seen a flock of huge crows, covering the vines with their wings to protect them from frost and hail. All that is utter nonsense and completely untrue. This is my secret: when I bought this vineyard it was planted with unsuitable varieties. Everything had been neglected. I went along to Monsieur d'Hargicourt, the proprietor of Château Margaux, and asked him for good varieties for my vineyards. This neighbour was kind enough to accede to my requests and was prepared to help me with his advice. I tended my vines as they do at Château Margaux and by the same methods I have obtained wines more or less the equal of those of my noble superior. So now, you know my secret. Profit from it so that the vines of Margaux can make the best wines in the world." And it was so. From that day on, all the small proprietors of the commune had a hand in this wizardry. And to recall the enchantment which protected the vines of Rauzan-Gassies, the label bears two magic wings.

The wine of Rauzan-Gassies can be clearly distinguished from that of its neighbour, Rausan-Ségla. It has more body and substance and a robust constitution, resulting in rather less finesse. Sometimes a certain earthy flavour can be detected which surprises the taster with its violence but which disappears with time and changes into lively, powerful aromas. More sturdy and forceful in its early youth than other Margaux wines, Rauzan-Gassies has a strong personality which cannot leave you indifferent. Bearing in mind what I said about Rausan-Ségla, I think that of this couple it is Rauzan-Gassies which wears the trousers, but they can be of velvet or sometimes of silk. And then you have trousers suited to great occasions.

Saint-Jacques (Château) → Siran

Saint-Marc (Château)

Commune: Soussans. **Proprietor:** Marc Faure. **Size of vine-yard:** 7 hectares. **Average age of vines:** 25 years. **Varieties:** 2/3 cabernet, 1/3 merlot. **Production:** 20,000 bottles CB. **Direct sales and by mail order:** Château Saint-Marc, Soussans, 33460 Margaux. Tel. 56 88 30 67. **Marketing:** through the trade.

Marc Faure has been the proprietor of Saint-Marc since 1958. He inherited the larger part of the vineyard, but several purchases over the last twenty years have brought the area up to 7 hectares, which is far from being negligible in the Margaux AOC.

Cultivation and vinification are traditional... even a very model of conservatism. The wines have character with a wide range of savours, a fact which is explained by the different variety of soils: gravel, sandy gravel, clayey chalk and silicious. A long fermentation period gives them a high tannin content, which results in rather less suppleness but greater fullness and power. They are wines which deserve to be aged for several years after being bottled.

Siran (Château)

Commune: Labarde. **Proprietor:** William-Alain B. Miailhe, assisted by E. Thérasse. **Size of vineyard:** 35 hectares. **Average age of vines:** 38 years. **Varieties:** 50% cabernet-sauvignon, 25% merlot, 15% petit-verdot, 10% cabernet-franc. **Production:** 150,000 bottles CB. **Direct sales and by mail order:** Château Siran, 6 quai Louis XVIII, BP 35, 33024 Bordeaux Cedex. Tel. 56 81 35 01 or 56 88 34 04. **Marketing:** occasionally through the trade.

Like its neighbour Dauzac, the estate of Siran was dependent on the rural town-ship of Sainte-Croix (*see* Dauzac) straddling the parishes of Macau and Labarde where, in the fifteenth century, lived a certain Guilhem de Siran Esq., a vassal of Sainte-Croix. Like the majority of estates in the Médoc, Siran went through diffi-cult times during the Revolution, the then proprietor, Count de La Roque Bouillac, having emigrated in 1791. His daughter Jeanne managed to make ends meet by marrying Alphonse, Count de Toulouse-Lautrec. They had a grandson called Henri, who was the well-known artist.

Like several unfortunate *crus*, Siran was overlooked by the classification of 1855. And yet it was highly esteemed in the eighteenth century and a classification in 1848 mentions among the fourth *crus* the wine of Bellegarde, which belonged to the famous Count J.-B. Lynch. Bellegarde is the name of a gravelly plateau in Labarde which belongs to the estate of Siran today, and the Bellegarde label is that of the second wine of the *cru*. It was in 1848 that Monsieur Léo Barbier bought Château 177

The vat-house at Château Siran is as fine as those of the grands crus classés.

Siran. For nearly two centuries, the Barbiers-Miailhes, who came from Portets in the department of Gironde, were great wine-brokers.

The Miailhe family are descended from the Barbiers and have become one of the most famous, if sometimes contentious, clans in the Médoc. Of the present generation, May-Eliane de Lencquesaing, famous as "Madame la Générale", has done much to restore the fortunes of Pichon Longueville Comtesse de Lalande. In the share-out of the family, her brother William-Alain became proprietor of Siran. His undisguised ambition is to place Siran in the ranks of the *crus classés*. This may come about in time. Meanwhile, he has created a model, highly visitor-conscious estate. Its trim, well-kept appearance fits felicitously into the landscape of Labarde.

The colour of the working buildings (cellars, vat-houses, workers' living quarters, etc.) is pink ("la vigne en rose", as it were) and a few surprises await the visitor. First of all, there is a heliport constructed on the flat roof of the cellars next to huge reception rooms. There is a little tower lined with cabinets filled with oriental china of the eleventh to fifteenth centuries and finally there is an anti-nuclear vintage wine shelter whose imposing metal-screened door carries a plaque with the inscription: "Better red than dead", to ensure a satisfactory continuation of the ageing process in the eventuality of atomic disaster. Alain Miailhe is a lover of history and a great collector. He has gathered together a multitude of objects relating to vines and wines and he has a faithful reconstruction of the viticultural Land Register of the

Formerly, the châteaux by the riverside had their port. Siran has its heliport.

Margaux appellation as at 1828, executed by a team from Bordeaux University under the direction of Professor Pijassou. This document would be useful for the experts if ever there were any question of a new classification....

Imitating Philippe de Rothschild, Alain Miailhe has the labels of Siran painted by contemporary artists. All this does not make Siran a better wine, but simply goes to show how open-minded the proprietor is. He is interested in mankind and its story. Professor Emile Peynaud comes from time to time to Siran to check that the recent vintages are developing correctly. Over the last years, Siran has produced very successful wines. They are generally very aromatic, brawny, vinous and round in the mouth. They can certainly not claim that extreme distinction which is to be found in the communes of Margaux and Cantenac, but sometimes we prefer this type of cordiality to the fine manners of insubstantial lords.

Soussans (Château) ⚱→ *Deyrem-Valentin*

Tayac (Château)

cru bourgeois

Commune: Soussans. **Proprietor:** André Favin. Estate manager: Madame Portet. **Size of vineyard:** 34 hectares. **Average age of vines:** 18 years. **Varieties:** 70% cabernet-sauvignon and cabernet-franc, 25% merlot, 5% petit-verdot. **Production:** 200,000 bottles CB. **Direct sales and by mail order:** in France and abroad. André Favin, Tayac, Soussans, 33460 Margaux. Tel. 56 88 33 06. **Marketing:** through the trade; Savour Club, Maison Ginestet, Maison Lebègue.

The late André Favin was the owner of Château Tayac since 1960 and until quite recently. With its 34 hectares of vines, it is at one and the same time the largest of the small and the smallest of the large estates. It covers a large area on the plateau of the village of Tayac which depends on Soussans on the extreme northwest of the Margaux appellation. The terrain is of sandy gravel with a subsoil of clayey chalk. At the beginning of the century, Château Tayac had only 18 hectares of vines and Féret classed it among the *crus bourgeois* and 1st *artisans*, mentioning that this vineyard was likely to increase. At the time, the Margaux appellation had not been delimited and the estate of Tayac spilled over into Avensan and Moulis. There was a certain production of wines from the loamy soils which was not to the benefit of the *cru*'s reputation. At the end of the nineteenth century, vinification at Tayac was carried out by M. Mellet, the proprietor of Dubignon-Talbot. In 1892, the estate was split up. The Larauza family reunited it recently. André Favin was a capable grower who taught himself the science of wine-making by natural osmosis. From planting to tasting, he knew everything. But he had two professional activities, for he was also a builder. As such he was responsible for several extensions to or constructions of cellars in the Margaux AOC, notably those of Prieuré-Lichine. Belying the proverb which says that it is the shoemaker's wife who is always the worst shod, he gave his *cru* functional and modern installations which are very agreeable to visit. The wines are as robust as André Favin was himself. Nor are they lacking in joviality or a delicate natural finesse.

The late André Favin among his wines.

Tayac-Plaisance (Château)

Commune: Soussans. **Proprietor:** Paul Bajeux, who manages and runs the estate. **Size of vineyard:** 2 hectares. **Average age of vines:** 30 years. **Varieties:** 20% cabernet-sauvignon, 65% merlot, 15% cabernet-franc and petit-verdot. **Production:** 12,000 bottles CB. **Direct sales and by mail order:** Paul Bajeux, Tayac, Soussans, 33460 Margaux. Tel. 56 88 36 83. **Marketing:** through the trade.

Tayac-Plaisance is Paul Bajeux's hobby when he is not busy with his small firm which builds most of the family vaults in the neighbourhood. This little parcel of vines is a family inheritance which he tends, renews and enlarges from year to year. Its petit-verdot is one of the oldest in Soussans. Paul Bajeux's vineyard produces a wine which ranks in good place with the best *crus artisans* in the Margaux appellation. In practice, Paul Bajeux will not sell his wine to any outsiders because he has too many friends queuing up. But if you decide to build a tomb anywhere around Margaux, you may have a chance to become a new customer.

Tertre (Château du)

5e cru classé

Commune: Arsac. **Proprietor:** Société du Château du Tertre. **Director:** Philippe Capbern-Gasqueton. **Manager:** Alain de Baritault. **Size of vineyard:** 48 hectares. **Average age of vines:** 25 years. **Varieties:** 65% cabernet-sauvignon and cabernet-franc, 30% merlot, 5% petit-verdot. **Production:** 200,000 bottles CB. **Sales by mail order:** Château du Tertre, Arsac, 33460 Margaux. Tel. 56 59 30 08. **Marketing:** 4/5 through the trade, and sales to individual customers.

The gravelly slopes of Château du Tertre rise to some seventy-two feet in height. They are in the commune of Arsac which is the highest in the Margaux appellation. The subsoil is ferruginous and of limestone which gives the wines of Le Tertre an individual character, rather resembling those of the Bordeaux Graves.

When Thomas, the brother of Michel de Montaigne, married Jacquette d'Arsac, he took a great step forward, acquiring considerable stretches of land in the Médoc. He was also a proprietor on the Atlantic Coast to the south of Soulac, near the peninsula of La Négade in Lilhan. But there, he and his vines lost their footing for the estate was completely submerged by the Atlantic and its dunes: "Along the Médoc coast, my brother, Lord d'Arsac, has seen one of his estates buried under the sand thrown up by the sea", wrote Montaigne to La Boétie. The two brothers and their friends used to meet at Château La Tour Carnet in Saint-Laurent, where their sister Madeleine, the wife of Thibaut de Camin, used to live. The Ségur family owned Le Tertre in the eighteenth century. Along with Château d'Arsac it was then a single huge estate which was split up at the time of the Revolution. Afterwards, it passed successively into the hands of Brézet, Henry, Vallandé, Koenigswarter and Bernheim. The thirties and the years of the Second World War were particularly detrimental to its interests. Philippe Capbern-Gasqueton, who is also the proprietor

Sloping vineyards at Château du Tertre for this "château on the knoll".

of Calon-Ségur in Saint-Estèphe, today runs Château du Tertre and its 48 hectares of vines in one unbroken stretch, which is rather rare for the *crus classés*. Moreover, Château du Tertre is the only *cru classé* in the commune of Arsac and, with Dauzac, is a fifth *cru* in the Margaux appellation. The restoration of the château is under way.

Treilles (Domaine des)

Commune: Soussans. **Proprietor:** Guy Nouaux. **Size of vineyard:** 0.35 hectares. **Average age of vines:** 40 years. **Varieties:** malbec, cabernet and merlot. **Production:** 1,800 bottles CB. **Direct sales and by mail order:** Domaine des Treilles, 1 rue Montaigne, 33460 Margaux. Tel. 56 88 31 54. **Marketing:** through the trade; Ets. Marcellin Marceau, Bordeaux.

At Marsac, Guy Nouaux is the proprietor of several rows of vines which have been there as long as his family, one of the oldest in the area. Moreover, everything is conducted in "the old style": replanting is done by layering the stock and replacement is considered only after its natural death (could Guy Nouaux's official job – he is Margaux's undertaker – be responsible for this pious respect for life?). This respect for tradition includes short pruning and the different ways of ploughing (he abandoned the horse just a short time ago), as well as fermentation, which is a real infusion of grape-skins in their own juice. The result is "bull's blood", that is to say a wine which is hellishly tannic and devilishly "munchy".

The casks are not often renewed, but what does that matter, for the wine takes its traditional personality from them and a slight degree of volatile acidity has never harmed anybody; on the contrary, it is good for sinusitis, pleurisy and dropsy, not to mention gout. So then, take a drop of Guy Nouaux's Domaine des Treilles; it is better than any tonic.

Trois Chardons (Château des)

Commune: Cantenac. **Proprietor:** Claude, Yves and Pierre Chardon. **Size of vineyard:** 2.20 hectares. **Average age of vines:** 30 years. **Varieties:** cabernet, merlot and petit-verdot. **Production:** 8,000 bottles CB. **Direct sales and by mail order:** M. Chardon, Issan, Cantenac, 33460 Margaux. Tel. 56 88 33 94.

It should first be said that the name, *trois chardons*, means "Three Thistles". Now let me introduce them: the father, Pierre Chardon, and his two sons, Claude and Yves, all tall and stalwart, with features chiselled by a billhook for pruning verdot. Their principal activity is directing Château Palmer where the Chardon family's presence is almost a tradition (already the two grandsons, Eric and Philippe, are working in the cellars and on the vines). They also consecrate their time to public service. Pierre Chardon, who was born at Palmer, is the honorary mayor of Cantenac, having administered the commune for thirty-three years. His son, Claude, is for the moment the deputy mayor. On Saturdays and Sundays, they look after their little vineyard which was formerly called the *cru* of the Grand-Caneyron. At harvest-time, relations, friends and neighbours come to give a hand. It is a festive occasion. And the prickly family motto announces a permanent invitation to all the Chardons' friends: "Qui s'y frotte... y repique!" (Whoso touches it... will be pricked anew). The wine of the Trois Chardons is rare because of its tiny production, but it is not a wine to prickle the palate. It is one of the best-produced *crus artisans* in all the Margaux appellation. Fine, elegant, feminine, highly perfumed, this wine which comes from a pocket handkerchief vineyard makes me think of an old Bordeaux broker who, whenever he came across a *cru* with a particularly pronounced bouquet, used to declare: "This wine is one suitable for perfuming handkerchiefs." But even if it were to be sold in aerosol sprays, there would not be enough for everybody.

Vallière (Château)

Commune: Soussans. **Proprietor:** Jean-Pierre Touya. **Size of vineyard:** 0.35 hectares. **Average age of vines:** 11 years. **Varieties:** traditional. **Production:** 1,800 bottles CB. **Direct sales:** M. J.-P. Touya, Virefougasse, Soussans, 33460 Margaux. Tel. 56 88 71 24.

Vallière's little vineyard by the side of Virefougasse, is a family estate which Jean-Pierre Touya cultivates when he has the time. The label of the *cru* is typical of a period when printers in Bordeaux produced a catalogue giving a choice of various picturesque scenes of the Gironde vineyards. The grower had the choice of twenty different scenes of harvesting, twelve of ploughing, fourteen of pretty girls at harvest, one hundred and forty pictures of châteaux and all the different ways of despatching casks of wine... by foot, by horse, by carriage and by sailing boat.

The Wetterwald Press, founded in 1815, was the first to produce labels for Bor-

deaux, in photogravure or in lithography. The label of Château Vallière bears the

number 224 in the Wetterwald catalogue. It is almost a collector's item, of extremely limited edition, for Jean-Pierre Touya harvests about one-and-a-half tonneaux per year. That is six hogsheads. He ages his wine in casks used only once by the *grands crus*. Jean-Pierre Touya is a typical good vigneron.

Vieux Cep (Cru du)

The 0.1026 hectares of vines of the Cru du Vieux Cep was uprooted in 1983 by its proprietor, Jean Joyeux, who is today a retired man living in Margaux after being the third generation of estate managers at Château Rausan-Ségla. Planted by his grandfather, these vines were older than himself. I take it as a small-scale example of the names of *crus* which have disappeared over the generations and centuries. A great number of *crus bourgeois, artisans* and *paysans* have been absorbed by larger estates. Sometimes the label is kept alive for the second wine of a *cru classé*. Sometimes it falls into the darkness of oblivion. From time to time, one of them reappears in a salesroom catalogue when someone has died leaving a cellar to be put up at auction. The châteaux, often beautiful mansions from the end of the nineteenth century, have now become strictly residential. To speak only of the commune of Margaux, we can mention Abel-Laurent, Doumens, Lamouroux, Lestonnat, La Tour de l'Aubion, La Gombeaude, La Colonilla, Richet-Marian.

Vincent (Château)

cru bourgeois supérieur

Commune: Cantenac. **Proprietor:** Madame Jean Domec. The estate is run by La Société du Château Palmer. **Size of vineyard:** 5 hectares. **Average age of vines:** 25 years. **Varieties:** traditional. **Production:** 15,000 bottles. **Direct sales and by mail order:** Château Vincent, Cantenac, 33460 Margaux. Tel. 56 88 30 12.

185

We have already seen the name of Jadouin mentioned as an important family of proprietors in the Margaux appellation and, more particularly, at Cantenac and Arsac. One of the daughters of Jules Jadouin married a Lebègue and the other, a Boiteau. (Lebègue, in French, being suggestive of stammering, and Boiteau of lameness, they were easy prey to facile witticisms by the locals.) Then later, a Boiteau daughter married Adolphe Domec, a master glass-blower in Bordeaux. In the eighteenth century, such crafts were well represented in the Bacalan quarter by the pottery of Vieillard (and Johnston) and the Domec glass-works.

With its pretty little garden of flowers and its tiny country house straight out of an operetta, Château Vincent is one of the prettiest dwellings in the area. Madame Jean Domec has a charming antique shop in Paris at number 40, rue Mazarine, selling items of the *belle époque,* but she gladly leaves the capital to spend short visits at Vincent, which is situated between Montbrun and Palmer. It is Château Palmer which runs the five hectares of vines attached to the property. Rent is paid in kind, and after the attentive vinification of the Chardons, the wine ages in casks in the cellars of Château Vincent, where bottling is also carried out. Martine Domec lacks neither friends nor relations and all her production finds its way into a large closed circle. You can try to break into it; you will be in good company.

Vincent: a doll's house for a great little wine.

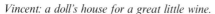

Annexes

A brief history of the Margaux appellation since its creation

Vintage	Production (ha)	Production (hl)	Production (hl/ha)	Success of vintage	Ageing potential	Remarks
1955	656	18,148	27.65	●●●●○	◇◇	Several crus suffered from hailstorms. Certain bottles are remarkable.
1956	609	7,739	12.70	●○		Charming wines can still be found today.
1957	570	7,924	13.89	●●●	◇◇	A hard year with high acidity which risks "dying" before maturing.
1958	538	8,627	16.02	●●○	◇	Several châteaux are delicious. For example, Palmer.
1959	610	12,868	21.10	●●●○	◇◇	The average standard of quality is not up to its reputation.
1960	613	16,337	26.65	●●○		Château Margaux is astonishing. Wines to be drunk.
1961	610	7,257	11.90	●●●●●	◇◇◇◇	A "year of the century" for bottles a hundred years old.
1962	634	16,069	25.36	●●●○	◇◇	A good year with a depth of acidity.
1963	676	23,461	34.68	●		You can sip two or three.
1964	715	28,585	40	●●○○	◇	Very irregular in quality. A few successes. Some disappointments.
1965	724	21,817	30.14	○		Best forgotten.
1966	757	22,197	29.33	●●●○	◇◇	Today preferable to the 67s, in my opinion.
1967	801	29,862	37.31	●●●●	◇◇	Well-structured wines, but rather hard.
1968	837	21,806	26.05	○		None to be found.
1969	864	17,530	20.29	●●○	◇	Often disappointing.
1970	908	35,492	39.06	●●●●○	◇◇◇	A good year which should still be kept.
1971	899	19,675	21.88	●●●○	◇◇	Much better than their reputation. Delicious today.
1972	893	24,278	27.18	●○		Some people like them chilled.
1973	912	38,474	42.20	●●●○	◇◇	An all-round success. Very agreeable wines.
1974	894	39,488	44.18	●●○	◇	A few rare successes in an average standard.
1975	936	27,173	29.03	●●●●●	◇◇◇◇◇	Still closed up, they cannot claim to be in the category of the 61s but it is a pity to drink them now.
1976	988	37,674	38	●○○	◇	Will gain nothing with further ageing. A rather good year.
1977	1,050	21,849	21	●●	◇◇◇	A strong fixed acidity but generally disappointing.
1978	1,036	34,137	33	●●●○○	◇◇	A great year. Very supple. Ready for drinking.
1979	1,052	49,373	47	●●●●	◇◇◇	A very good year which deserves to be kept a little longer.
1980	1,052	34,048	32	●●○	◇	Rather light. Wines for lunch.
1981	1,065	43,300	40.65	●●●○	◇◇◇◇	A good year which should improve.
1982	1,101	60,770	55	●●●●○	◇◇◇◇◇	Will be long talked of, an exceptional year.
1983	1,146	58,372	50	●●●●●	◇◇◇◇◇◇	The greatest success since 61. Outstanding.
1984	1,177	40,974	34.81	●○○	◇◇	Rather light, delicate wines which will not age well.
1985	1,198	62,619	52.26	●●●●○	◇◇◇◇◇◇	Fully ripe grapes. All the crus were very successful.
1986	1,209	63,031	52.13	●●●●○	◇◇◇◇◇◇	No coulure. Same characteristics as 1985. Ripe, concentrated tannins.
1987	1,214	57,048	46.99	●●●	◇◇◇◇◇	A vintage with hardly any merlot. Austere wines which will develop slowly.
1988	1,242	57,317	46.15	●●●●●●	◇◇◇◇◇◇	A very great year. Huge wines which should become magnificent. Finesse and fullness.

The table denotes the evolution of the area under production and the yields obtained. Note that the number of hectolitres produced per hectare is not always inversely proportionate to the quality of the wine (e.g. 11.9 hectolitres in 1961, 39.06 in 1970, and 50 in 1983).
The total number of circles indicates the relative success of the vintage. The number of black circles indicates if the wines are more or less full-bodied.
The indication as to potential ageing presumes a vintage's future calculated from the present time. Certain years are "dead".
A rectangle corresponds to a period of between three to five years. So, a vintage noted with 4 rectangles can hope to have a life-span of from 12 to 20 years.

Index of proprietors

Picture acknowledgements:

Château Cantenac-Brown (106); Alain Danvers (78, 82); Château Giscours–Aérovue Diffusion, Mérignac (116); Luc Joubert, Bordeaux (20, 24, 52, 72, 73, 74, 144, 188); Château Labégorce-Zédé–Photo Thienpont (129); Château Lascombes (135); Domaine de Maucaillou (157); Michel Plassart, Paris (49); Scope–Michel Guillard, Paris (cover, 16, 147, 148); Château Siran (178, 180); Wetterwald (185); Claude Lada and Douglas Metzler, for the rest of the book.